A MOHAVE WAR
REMINISCENCE
1854-1880

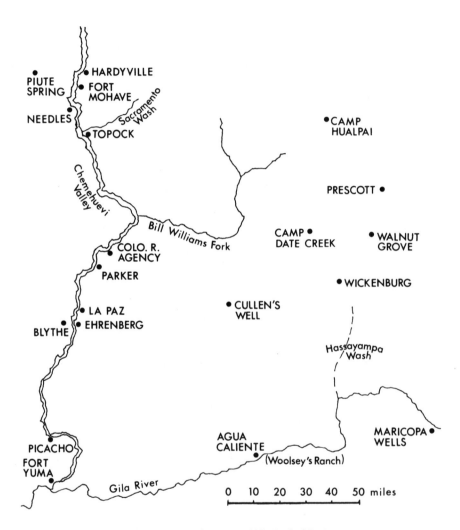

PIUTE
SPRING
● HARDYVILLE
● FORT
MOHAVE
NEEDLES ●
Sacramento Wash
● TOPOCK
●CAMP
HUALPAI
Chemehuevi Valley
PRESCOTT ●
Bill Williams Fork
CAMP ●
DATE CREEK
● WALNUT
GROVE
● COLO. R.
AGENCY
● PARKER
● WICKENBURG
● LA PAZ
● CULLEN'S
WELL
BLYTHE ●● EHRENBERG
Hassayampa Wash
MARICOPA
WELLS ●
PICACHO
FORT
YUMA
AGUA
CALIENTE ●
(Woolsey's Ranch)
Gila River

0   10   20   30   40   50 miles

After Territories of New Mexico and Arizona; U.S. Chief of Engineers,
U.S. Army, 1879.   (U.S. National Archives copy)

A MOHAVE WAR REMINISCENCE 1854-1880

A. L. Kroeber
and
C. B. Kroeber

DOVER PUBLICATIONS, INC.
New York

Published in Canada by General Publishing Company, Ltd., 30
Lesmill Road, Don Mills, Toronto, Ontario.
Published in the United Kingdom by Constable and Company, Ltd.,
3 The Lanchesters, 162-164 Fulham Palace Road, London W6 9ER.

Bibliographical Note

This Dover edition, first published in 1994, is an unabridged
republication of the work first published by The University of
California Press, Berkeley, in 1973, as Volume 10 in the University of
California Publications in Anthropology Series. It is published by
special arrangement with The Regents of the University of California, a
California Corporation, for The University of California Press, 2120
Berkeley Way, Berkeley, California 94720.

Library of Congress Cataloging-in-Publication Data

Kroeber, A. L. (Alfred Louis), 1876-1960.
  A Mohave war reminiscence, 1854-1880 / A.L. Kroeber and C.B.
Kroeber.
      p.   cm.
  Originally published: Berkeley : University of California Press,
1973, in series: University of California publications in anthropology,
v. 10.
  Includes bibliographical references.
  ISBN 0-486-28163-9
  1. Mohave Indians—Wars. 2. Mohave Indians—History—19th
century. I. Kroeber, Clifton B. II. Title.
E99.M77K75 1994
399'.089'975—dc20   94-9162
                                                                      CIP

Manufactured in the United States of America
Dover Publications, Inc., 31 East 2nd Street, Mineola, N.Y. 11501

CONTENTS

Preface vii
Abbreviations Used in the Notes ix
Variations in the Spelling of Indian Names x
1. Introduction 1
2. Narrative of Chooksa homar
    Episode 1. War with the Cocopa: Captives 7
    Episode 2. First Conflict with Americans 11
    Episode 3. Peace Made with the Maricopa 14
    Episode 4. Second Conflict with Americans 18
    Episode 5. The First Soldiers Arrive 19
    Episode 6. The Soldiers Arrive in Force 20
    Episode 7. Peaceful Relations with the Military 24
    Episode 8. The Captive Mohave Escape 25
    Episode 9. Open War with the American Troops 27
    Episode 10. Peace and Return 32
    Episode 11. War with Yavapai and Walapai 34
    Episode 12. War with the Chemehuevi 39
    Episode 13. Acceptance of Law 46
3. Discussions
    Episode 1. War with the Cocopa: Captives 49
    Episode 2. First Conflict with Americans 52
    Episode 3. Peace Made with the Maricopa 54
    Episode 4. Second Conflict with Americans 60
    Episode 5. The First Soldiers Arrive 62
    Episode 6. The Soldiers Arrive in Force 63
    Episode 7. Peaceful Relations with the Military 67
    Episode 8. The Captive Mohave Escape 67
    Episode 9. Open War with the American Troops 68
    Episode 10. Peace and Return 69
    Episode 11. War with Yavapai and Walapai 72
    Episode 12. War with the Chemehuevi 82
    Episode 13. Acceptance of Law 89
Conclusions 92
Plates 99
Maps 1 and 2, reproduced from
    A. L. Kroeber, *A Mohave Historical Epic*,
    University of California Publications in
    Anthropological Records, 11:2 (Berkeley, 1951)   Inside Back Cover

PREFACE

IN 1958 WHEN I was visiting at home, my father Alfred Kroeber asked me whether I would like to collaborate with him in the final stages of editing a Mohave war reminiscence. He said that he wanted to try to discover the dates of various episodes in the document, to tell how exact the narrator's memory had been. He had never had time to go into published works or manuscripts which might help to date those episodes. He had substantially finished the work an anthropologist could do on this manuscript and now, he said, he "needed a historian." I took him up on it and started the reading necessary for one who had never looked into Arizona history and who knew nothing about southwestern Indians. Alfred and I had half a dozen conferences and a regular correspondence over the next two years until his death, but I went too slowly then to find all the questions I would like to ask him now. So this collaboration is of two parts—his work done mostly during the late 1940s and 1950s, and mine mostly since 1960.

Alfred had spent parts of two days in 1903 talking with a Mohave known to him as Jo Nelson, whom he took to be about sixty to sixty-five years of age at the time. Listening to Nelson through a Mohave interpreter, Jack Jones, Sr. (Quichnailk), Kroeber heard Nelson narrate his account of the wars in which the Mohave had engaged in Nelson's lifetime. Kroeber had asked the narrator to speak of those things he knew of his own knowledge, not through hearsay. The elderly Quichnailk was a most intelligent and alert man who would listen to as much as he could translate all at once—sentences, or a paragraph or more—and then would pass that much on to Kroeber, in English, Kroeber copying it down with his standard equipment of a yellow pencil and yellow pad of paper. There was some questioning by both Quichnailk and Kroeber, to fill in names or locations, or to clarify something else in detail; but I do not believe they guided the narrator in any way, or that Kroeber did anything to reshape the narrative afterward. In later years Kroeber went on to identify many of the place names mentioned by Nelson—whose mature Mohave name was Chooksa homar, I now know thanks to Lorraine Sherer's inquiry. Kroeber tried to identify any seeming obscurities in the narrative that referred to Mohave culture.

On the historical side Alfred had had very good advice from Professor Edward Howes of Sacramento State College, as to how to locate and use published and unpublished United States government records. He had had considerable help from Victor Gondos, Jr., Dr. Mabel E. Deutrich, and others in the National Archives of the United States. They had found some important manuscripts and furnished him copies, although they could not of course search out all the manuscripts Kroeber needed. To make a long story short, since 1958 I have been taking available time to read, and to visit libraries and archives, in an effort to run down some of the mysterious references in the reminiscence, and to date all the episodes if possible. After more than a month in the National Archives during summer, 1970, the search finally played out, still leaving mysteries, unidentified episodes, and other anomalies, as will be seen in the footnotes and Discussions below.

As for the authorship of our supporting material, all anthropological footnotes are Kroeber's; almost all referring to white mens' source materials are mine: and I wrote the Discussions and the introduction save where Kroeber is quoted. Wherever in the notes "we" assert something it means that Alfred and I both arrived at the conviction, each in his own way. Those who have not read Kroeber's contributions and texts from Mohave culture will find all but one listed in Ann J. Gibson and John H. Rowe, "A Bibliography of the Publications of Alfred Louis Kroeber," *American Anthropologist*, 63 (October, 1961), now adding *More Mohave Myths* which was issued by the University of California Press, in the Anthropological Records series, in 1972.

I have incurred obligations to many people. Professor Robert F. Heizer gave me important help in several different ways including temporary loan of some Kroeber manuscripts, and I am most grateful for his encouragement. For their watchful and most friendly guidance I wish to thank James B. Walker and Elmer Oris Parker, professional archivists in the National Archives; Yndia S. Moore (then Historical Secretary) and Dr. Ray Brandes (then Historian) in the Arizona Pioneers' Historical Society, Tucson; and Dr. Gilbert Dorame at the Federal Records Center, Bell, California. I am deeply grateful to Dr. Bernard L. Fontana, Ethnologist in the Arizona State Museum and member of the Department of Anthropology, the University of Arizona. Dr. Lorraine Sherer, professor emerita in the University of California, Los Angeles, urged me on, did much to help me avoid errors, and set an enviable standard of scholarship; and I am deeply grateful to her. The work has been much advanced by thoughtful assistance of research staffs and librarians in the Huntington Library, San Marino, California; the History Department of Los Angeles Public Library; the Sharlot Hall Museum, Prescott, Arizona; the University of Arizona Library; the Bancroft Library of the University of California, Berkeley; the Southwest Museum, Los Angeles; the Indian Claims Commission, Washington, D.C.; and Clapp Library, Occidental College, Los Angeles, whose Reference Librarian, John Saeger, has taught me a good deal. I wish to thank Arthur Woodward of Patagonia, Arizona, for his thoughtful help and encouragement; and Gail Helms for most acute proofreading and for preparing a beautiful typescript. A grant from the Research and Development fund of Occidental College helped a great deal toward the end; and during summer, 1970, at Washington, D.C. and in Los Angeles, I was beneficiary of a grant from the Wenner-Gren Foundation for Anthropological Research which alone made conclusion of the project feasible and for which I will always be grateful. Finally, this whole work is a much better thing than it was before Susan Peters of the University of California Press started out to edit the manuscript and see it through the press.

CLIFTON B. KROEBER

ABBREVIATIONS USED IN THE NOTES

AGO	Records of the Adjutant General's Office (a whole record group in U.S. National Archives, much of it now in microfilm publication).
APHS	Arizona Pioneers' Historical Society, Tucson, Arizona.
234	Letters Received by the Office of Indian Affairs, 1824-1881 (Microcopy 234, a microfilm publication of U.S. National Archives).
393	Records of United States Continental Army Commands, 1816-1920 (a whole record group in U.S. National Archives, now mostly published on microfilm).
617	Returns from U.S. Military Posts, 1800-1916 (Microcopy 617, a microfilm publication of U.S. National Archives).
734	Records of the Arizona Superintendency of Indian Affairs, 1863-1873 (Microcopy 734, a microfilm publication of U.S. National Archives).
Report, Indian Affairs	Annual report of the U.S. Commissioner of Indian Affairs, for the year specified (published at Washington, D.C.).
Report, War	Annual report of the U.S. Secretary of War for the year specified (published at Washington, D.C.)
UCPAAE	University of California Publications in American Archaeology and Ethnology (Berkeley, California).
USNA	United States National Archives and Record Service, Washington, D.C.

VARIATIONS IN THE SPELLING OF INDIAN NAMES

As-pan-ku-yah	Espanqua, Pan Coyer
Asukit	Asakita, Askit, Asakyet, Asoschet, Sicket, perhaps Sukiyet
Cairook	Keruk, Avi-havasuts, Avi-havasuch
Ho-mar-rah-tav	Homaratow, Homororow, Ho marrt tow
Homose-quahote	Homose:kohot, Asikahota, Sickahoot, Sikahot
Ochocama	A hootch a kah mah, Hootch-icama
Qolho qorau	Kulho Kwira:u, Kulho Korau, Hookarow
Quashacama	Coshacama, Ashackama, Queschacameu, Khershacamow
Yara tav	Eechee yara tav; Iritaba; Ereteba; Arateve; Yereteive; Aritab; Yarate:va

Since no order has yet been imposed on the rendering of Indian names in English, it appears to be desirable to reflect the many variations to be found in historical sources and in the scholarly literature. These variations occur for several reasons. Anglo-Americans set down different phonetic equivalents of names spoken to them by Indians—and Indians of different tribes often have slightly different versions of the same name. Sometimes too, only part of the name was in common use: thus, A. L. Kroeber in 1903 heard "Arateve," while George Devereux in 1938 transcribed "Yarate:va," whereas in the 1960s Lorraine Sherer heard the whole name "Eechee yara tav." Also, a Mohave man might use several names during his lifetime, and this is seen above for Cairook.

A MOHAVE WAR
REMINISCENCE
1854-1880

CHAPTER 1

INTRODUCTION

MOHAVE WARFARE: MOTIVATIONS, ENMITIES, AND AMITIES

WE KNOW too little of the life of the Mohave as it was before the Spaniards came into the American Southwest. Few Spaniards visited the tribe from the mid-sixteenth through the early nineteenth centuries, and very few left any account of the life of that Indian nation. The Spaniards no doubt influenced the culture of the Aha macave indirectly through other tribes, but knowledge of changes during the Spanish centuries remains speculative. Only in the 1820s did direct reports of the tribal customs begin to come from beaver-trapping expeditions that passed up or down the Colorado River. These reports are fragmentary. Mohave life begins to be better known with the United States government's exploring expeditions of the 1850s, several of which passed through Mohave Valley and left more comprehensive reports.

If we can assume a certain Spanish cultural influence, its effect must have been weak. Ethnologists visiting the tribe shortly after 1900 and from then until the 1950s did not report any notable Spanish or Mexican influences. They—Kroeber, Spier, Stewart, Fathauer, Devereux, Wallace, and a few more—seem to have assumed that the life they observed was much as it had been in aboriginal time, changed mainly after the beginning of Anglo-American domination in 1859.

Thus, the question does arise as to which chronological period of Mohave history is represented by the picture drawn in the ethnographers' reports. I doubt that they worried their heads much about this question, since so many elements of the culture would not change from one decade to another. Unfortunately these observers could not take enough time to do both ethnography and ethnohistory. They did reconstruct a very detailed picture of Mohave material life, and they preserved some of the literary-religio-historical texts, dreams, and song cycles which the Mohave had been recreating in oral form in each generation.

The older people, who knew the socio-economic and political "history" of the tribe prior to 1850, and who could also narrate the texts, were dying off in the years just before and soon after 1900. Ethnography done in the 1930s, 1940s, and 1950s had then to depend upon a few sons and daughters, but mostly on grandsons and granddaughters, of the last generation of independent Mohave. And their information was in some respects vague, incomplete, or conflicting.

With all the old people gone, and with very few written sources dating from before the 1850s, we still have no ethnohistorical study of how the tribal culture changed during its last independent generation. Such a lack of historical background makes it almost impossible to answer some of the basic questions about Mohave warfare. And there is little enough direct testimony to the war usages as they were even during the 1850s and 1860s, up to 1870 when this tribe's hostilities with other peoples came to an end.

We do know some of the influences that could have brought about rapid changes in Mohave life during the first half of the nineteenth century, but we do not know how deep the impact of those influences was. Almost all that is written about Mohave warfare comes from members of the tribe who were born too late—too late ever to have seen a Mohave war expedition going off to attack another tribe.

My own feeling is that the information given by the grandsons and granddaughters is particularly sound and complete as relates to the material things: weapons, decorations, and equipment, and is likely also complete as to ceremonial rites associated with warfare, some of which ceremonies survived in the tribe after warfare itself was done. But I would have doubts about the descriptions by descendants of Mohave warriors of the social aspects of war and some procedures followed while the men were out on the long expeditions. As for motivations of Mohave warfare the narrators have said very little, probably because they were not asked about it. A controversy has grown up around this question, which it will be well to review briefly as background to the narrative of Chooksa homar.

The ethnographers' viewpoint on why Mohave went to war is well phrased by George Fathauer who, after discussing various possibilities, summarized as follows. Mohave warfare was "non-instrumental," he thought: and "Such individual motivations of Mohave warfare as boredom, obsessive behavior, revenge, or the desire for prestige do not satisfactorily explain tribal wars. These motives were expressions of the basic magico-religious system which must be regarded as the primary cause of Mohave warfare although, of course, warfare in turn strengthened and reinforced the 'nationalistic' religion."[1] This echoes what Daryll Forde had found among the Yuma: "Fighting was not justified merely as a virile pursuit, nor was economic need adduced as a factor: warfare to the Yuma possessed a strong mystical value as the means whereby the spiritual power of the entire tribe was enhanced and at the same time demonstrated."[2] A. L. Kroeber thought they "fought for pleasure . . . an aggressive people thirsting for adventure and glory:" and that unlike other California Indians "feuds of locality and inherited revenge have given way . . . to a military spirit."[3] Kroeber hinted at an explanation of the origins of Mohave war, saying that the Mohaves' frequent journeyings into other peoples' territories "brought with them friendships and alliances as well as enmities . . . these belligerencies led them into hostile or amicable relations with people with whom they had but few direct contacts."[4]

So, long before the Anglo-Americans came on the scene the Mohave had a habit of aggressive warfare, which was being carried on within alignments of

---

[1] "The Structure and Causation of Mohave Warfare," *Southwestern Journal of Anthropology*, 10 (Spring, 1954), 97-118: see especially pp. 110,115.

[2] C. Daryll Forde, *Ethnography of the Yuma Indians*, University of California Publications in American Archaeology and Ethnology, 28 (Berkeley, 1931), p. 161 [hereinafter cited as UCPAAE].

[3] Kroeber, *Handbook of the Indians of California* (Washington, D.C., 1925), pp. 731, 728, and 727 respectively. Leslie Spier wrote that the Mohave viewed warfare as "nationalized sport": in *Cultural Relations of the Gila River and Lower Colorado Tribes*, Yale University Publications in Anthropology, 3 (New Haven, 1936), 5; and Kenneth Stewart is in accord in "Mohave Warfare," *Southwestern Journal of Anthropology*, 3 (Summer, 1947), 257-278.

[4] *Handbook*, p. 727.

"amities and enmities,"[5] among various tribes. By about 1830 this "far-stretching and interlocking line-up," as A. L. Kroeber termed it, found the Mohave as traditional enemies of the Pima-Maricopa and the Cocopa, attacking and raiding against those tribes alone or, at times in company with the Yuma, some bands of Yavapai, and sometimes with some Apache. So much for war against enemies living at a distance.

Near home, before 1830 the Mohave had ejected from their sections of the Colorado River lowlands those smaller Yuman tribes that had been living there. Into these empty lands filtered the Chemehuevi, from the desert west of the river, and they farmed the river bottom both north and south of lands then occupied by Mohaves. There was no tradition of warfare at that time between Mohave and Chemehuevi, nor between the Mohave and the bands of Walapai that lived adjoining them on the east. In Chooksa homar's narrative we will see that these peaceable relationships with nearest neighbors did change, after the Yuma and Mohave had been conquered by Anglo-Americans and while the Walapai, Yavapai, and Chemehuevi still resisted conquest by the whites. So much for the motivations for war, and the customary alliance pattern, as seen by ethnographers.

A group of ethnohistorians has presented a very different interpretation of Mojave warfare, after extensive study of historical documents dating from both Spanish and Anglo-American periods of Southwestern history. They assume that indirect Spanish influences became important enough that the warfare of Yuman tribes "was considerably elaborated by the impact of Spanish intervention," long before the Anglo-Americans' arrival.[6] They concluded that motivations for Mohave warfare had not been well understood by some ethnographers. Some of the main themes they saw in Yuman hostilities against other peoples were cavalry warfare; raiding other tribes to take prisoners, who were then held or sold as slaves; horse theft; and economic warfare. In all, they felt that Spanish influence had introduced these new themes, and had intensified some others, such as vengeance raiding, that were of aboriginal origin.

Probably neither ethnographers nor ethnohistorians could have much confidence in their conclusions about why the Mohave went to war. Motivation

---

[5] The following discussion in the text is based on Kroeber, *Handbook,* p. 596, since later ethnographic and historical work has borne out the alignments mentioned there. Kroeber did not imply our kind of hard-edged treaty or alliance relationships. These tribes did not "send" war parties, insofar as is known; individuals joined in expeditions proposed by individual warriors or other leaders. Some tribes listed in the alignments never functioned in any unified, "national" sense anyway, but lived as lineage groups and bands, to which such collective names as Yavapai, Walapai, and Paiute, have been given. Thus I would think of Jack Forbes's statement of these alignments as far too formalized, speaking of a "Quechan League" and its opponents: see *Warriors of the Colorado. The Yumas of the Quechan Nation and Their Neighbors* (Norman, Okla., 1965), esp. pp. 80-82. Likewise, Henry F. Dobyns, Paul H. Ezell, and Greta S. Ezell, "Death of a People," *Ethnohistory,* 10 (Spring, 1963), 132-135, 137, liken these alignments to the modern nation-state system and speak of strategic objectives in view for one or other group of tribes. These are not useful analogies. But now Dobyns and Robert C. Euler, in *Wauba Yuma's People* . . . (Prescott, Ariz., 1970), most persuasively argue that the Pai (Walapai) were in all important respects a tribe, one which managed a unified military response to the deadly challenge by whites.

[6] Henry F. Dobyns, Paul H. Ezell, Alden W. Jones, and Greta Ezell, "Thematic Changes in Yuman Warfare," in *Cultural Stability and Cultural Change,* ed. Verne F. Ray (Seattle, Wash., 1947:

is a tricky thing to get at, for an individual or for a whole nation of people, and especially when the people themselves are gone. Remembering that there is no thorough-going written "history" of the Mohave up to the 1860s, the most anyone can do is to make guesses about it. If this is the case, I would prefer the ethnographers' explanations of why the Mohave went to war. Their views seem to rest upon two related assumptions. One of these is that warfare had long been imbedded in Mohave life as one of its most valued expressions. It had become an end in itself, something in life that members of the tribe looked forward to whether they themselves were or were not warriors. The second assumption is that Mohave warfare was an end in itself because it so closely embodied and identified with basic beliefs of the people as to their origins, their glorious past with all its vicissitudes, and the kind of people they took themselves to be. These may well be safe assumptions, both as to the role of war among the Mohave, and as to the high spirits in which they engaged in fighting other tribes.

The ethnohistorians' theory does not seem to me to fit so well the historical context of Mohave life, as best we know of it through bits and snatches of information dating from before the late 1850s. One assumption the ethnohistorians make is that Spanish influence, although indirect, was strong enough to accomplish basic changes in whatever had been the aboriginal war pattern. Another assumption seems to be that, once the Spanish impact had fully registered, later events merely intensified those same "themes," during the first half of the nineteenth century (those themes being cavalry warfare, horse theft, raiding for prisoners and sale of slaves, and economic raiding).

Those two assumptions do not seem to bear out, in light of the pitifully small amount of information now at hand. The Mohave owned and used horses, but I know of no instance up to the 1850s of their taking horses on war expeditions. Nor do I know of their raiding other tribes, or white settlements, for horses, until the United States Army had invaded Mohave Valley itself in 1859. As for slaving, the Mohave were great visitors and travelers, but seem to have traded rather little. Also, to be sure that the Mohave went to war so as to take prisoners, make slaves of them, and trade those slaves, one would need first to know that the Mohave went to war often. This we do not know. Likewise, we do not know that any large number of prisoners was brought home, from any one expedition. Nor is it clear that the Mohave traded prisoners as commodities, even when they had one, two, or a few more on hand.

The Mohave did take prisoners, but only women and sometimes children. From the very few instances on the record, it looks as if the prisoners had a prideful, symbolic meaning to the Mohave. They were intent on taking prisoners, no doubt; but where or when they traded these prisoners as slaves is not clear.

The same seems to be the case for economic raiding in general: After the 1820s there was nobody near at hand the Mohave wanted to attack, and I have not seen any record of their having brought back plunder from the long expeditions against the Cocopa or the Pima-Maricopa. The Mohave were indeed destructive when at war. They would burn dwellings, destroy crops, make off with a few

reprinted, 1969), p. 50. By the same authors, "What Were Nixoras?" *Southwestern Journal of Anthropology,* 16 (1960), 230-258: by Paul Ezell, *The Hispanic Acculturation of the Gila River Pimas,* Memoir 90. American Anthropological Association (Menasha, Wis., 1961): and other works by Dobyns, Paul Ezell, and Euler.

women and, presumably, with any horses they could take—although I have seen no record of their stealing horses while on a war party. There is no indication that any of this mayhem was committed so as to accumulate wealth. And the conduct of Mohave returning from war indicates that they came fast, on foot, suggesting that there would be very little if any booty they could carry with them across the desert.

It may be safer to assume that the Mohave lived at the far outer rim of Spanish cultural influence, receiving the horse but little else save distorted and vague influences from Spanish-Indian life elsewhere in the Southwest. The Anglo-Americans who first came among the Mohave do not seem to have found them trading slaves, nor fighting on horseback. I am not sure that they had steel knives. They could not speak even broken Spanish, although a very few of them may have started to speak bits of Spanish by the late 1850s. That they had been subject to some direct and some indirect Spanish-Mexican influences is indubitable; but that such influences had altered their motivations for war seems unlikely.

MOHAVE WARFARE: PROCEDURES, PANOPLY, AND RITUAL

In Chooksa homar's memoir we hear very little about the intricate usages of Mohave war, its weapons, the highly formalized roles of different leaders and followers, or the fiestas of celebration, ceremonies of mourning, and ritual purification rites, that were aftermaths of warmaking. Information of all these culture elements was gathered by ethnographers, and no doubt represents the old customs, probably as they were before 1830. Anyone reading Stewart's and Fathauer's articles and Leslie Spier's *Mohave Culture Items* may also feel with Spier that some of this ethnographic material, narrated by grandsons and great-granddaughters of the independent Mohave, had by the 1940s and 1950s begun here and there to represent "overformulation."[7] The narrators who talked with anthropologists at that late date had been born too late to have seen Mohave warfare as it was in the 1820s and the 1840s. My guess is that they somewhat overdescribed what was, admittedly, a very formal and intricate set of customs. But whether or not these ethnographic analyses are perfectly complete, or overly exact, they must reflect the Mohave war enterprise as it was on the offensive against other tribes. Much less is known of Mohave defensive warfare, perhaps because the Mohave seem hardly to have engaged in it before the 1850s.

To me, one of the mysteries of Chooksa homar's reminiscence is why he says so little about all the usages of offensive warfare. We will return to this question later.

MOHAVE WARFARE: THE UNWRITTEN HISTORY

It is a pity that no one has seen enough information to be able to write the history of the Mohave during their last generation of independence, a period of

---

[7] Spier, *Mohave Culture Items,* Museum of Northern Arizona, Bulletin no. 28 (Flagstaff, Ariz., 1955), esp. 11, 14.

time that is reflected in the early episodes of Chooksa homar's memoir. That last generation of freedom must have been turbulent, with new stimuli and challenges, a time of swift cultural change encountering strong resistance from attitudes and customs that were deeply rooted. For many years the Mohave had been safe in their valley. Their remaining enemies, the Cocopa and Maricopa, never came there to raid. Now the Mohave discovered what accurate gunfire could do against their hand-to-hand, club-wielding style of fighting. Now they could be surprised at any moment by small parties of enemies who had no nearby homeland and who came heavily armed on horseback. They saw camels and steamboats in Mohave Valley. They witnessed the gradual humiliation and subjection of their friends the Quechan. They heard that everywhere to the eastward the white man was subjecting the Indian. They had seen such a thing, even earlier, in coastal California. Near at hand, the white man was now making friends of other tribes, the Paiute to their northward and Pima in the south.

We do not know what the Mohave felt about all these new events and new relationships. Nor do we know how their customs of war may have changed after 1830, when they had only distant enemies to fight. It seems possible that they no longer took horses on campaign. By that time they may have felt other, preferred needs for the few horses they had.

What the feelings of the "common people" were, as to the desirability of war itself, we do not know. What the increased contact with white people was doing to Mohaves' views of property and its uses, we likewise cannot tell; although it is clear enough that they had not yet entered the money economy of the Southwest by 1859, any more than they had entered the idea world of Spanish, the lingua franca of the region. So, in presenting the narrative of Chooksa homar we have not been able to frame it with any comprehensive view of the cultural stress and strain that must have been of the essence of Mohave life as the 1830s gave way to the 1840s and 1850s, as Chooksa homar himself was born, and as a larger world began at last to send its outriders into the valley of the Aha macave.

CHAPTER 2

NARRATIVE OF CHOOKSA HOMAR

EPISODE 1. WAR WITH THE COCOPA: CAPTIVES

1. The Yuma were at war with the Cocopa [Kwikapa], who sent word to the Halyikwamai and Akwa'ala, from both of whom men came to help them against the Yuma. Then these sent word to the Mohave: "We were fighting the Cocopa and they have got two tribes as allies. They are too many for us: we are afraid." The Mohave said: "Good, we will come."[1]So a party went down river for ten days, reached the Cocopa, fought [with the Yuma] against them, and came home in twenty days.[2] I saw them start and return when I was a boy.[3]

2. They had killed three [Cocopa] men and taken two women prisoners. Back at Yuma, the Mohave said: "We were not looking for war. But the three tribes together were too many for you: that is why we came and fought.[4] Well, we have killed three men and taken two women. We will not leave the women here with you.[5] We want to take them home and give them to an old man. We want them to be married and perhaps have a child. When such a boy is grown, he may go down river [to the Cocopa] and cause fighting to stop and everything will be friendly then. That is why we want to take these women.[6] It is far to walk; perhaps they will become tired and thirsty and hungry and will die on the way;[7] nevertheless we will [try to] take them."

3. The Yuma chief, Pascual [Paskwãole],[8] said: "I know the soldiers near here are watching us. That is what they are here for: that we do not fight. But those

---

[1] They were traditional allies against Cocopa, and the Halchidhoma and other Maricopa; and these were events from recurrent Cocopa-Quechan hostilities of the early 1850s. See Jack Forbes, *Warriors of the Colorado* (Norman, Okla., 1965), pp. 325-338.

[2] Rounded: it took nearly ten days to reach Yuma. The Cocopa were a couple of days beyond; and there were conferences with the white garrison, no doubt, and among the allies (A.L.K.). I think that this occurred in early 1854 (C.B.K.).

[3] From his statement in the next episode, Chooksa homar would have been about five at the time.

[4] Justification to the white listener of 1903? Anyhow, the restatement of known facts is typical.

[5] See sections 13, 15, 16 below.

[6] This is the motive constantly alleged. It may have been partly true; but, primarily, captives were symbols of victory and occasions for festivity. Compare A. L. Kroeber, "Olive Oatman's Return," *Kroeber Anthropological Society Papers*, 4 (1951), 1-18.

[7] The Oatman story shows it was a hard trip for women: the pace was that of warriors.

[8] Kae-as-no-cum, born about 1800: see Capt. A. B. MacGowan to Supt. Herman Bendell, Fort Yuma, March 14, 1872, Records of the Bureau of Indian Affairs, Letters Received by the Office of Indian Affairs, 1824-1881, U.S. National Archives [the letters hereinafter cited as 234; the archive, as USNA]. Pascual was "appointed" head chief of the Quechan by Major Samuel P. Heintzelman on Oct. 23, 1852 (MacGowan, cit. supra); he had been a kwanami (Forbes, p. 323); it is not known when he became the titular chief of the Quechan. He was styled "the head chief of the Yumas" by Capt. Geo. H. Thomas, commanding Fort Yuma, in a report of Aug. 8, 1854: Records of the War Department, Records of the Quartermaster General. Fort Yuma, USNA.

Fort Yuma was reoccupied by army forces commanded by Heintzelman on Feb. 29, 1852: Post Return, Fort Yuma, Calif., Feb. 1852, Records of the War Department, Returns from U.S. Military

others attacked us, that is what made us angry, and we sent word to you and you came and helped us, and we killed three and took two captives.[9] So I will go and see the officer of the soldiers." So, near sundown, he went to him and told him everything that had happened.

4. The commandant said: "If people do no harm and only work and live, do not fight them. But if they kill, you may kill them. That is why we are here, to stop you all from fighting. Some tribes are bad, and if I say to you to fight them, then fight. But if I do not say so, then do not fight. Are the Mohave still here?"

5. Paskwāole said: "Yes." "Bring them here tomorrow. I want to tell them the same thing."

6. So Paskwāole returned and reported to the Mohave. The Mohave leader was Aratêve,[10] who died on the Parker Reservation not so very long ago. He said: "I did not wish to fight: it is bad. But you wanted me and sent for me. I would like to see the commandant. He is right. I don't want to fight. We will see tomorrow what he says. There are four or five of you [Mohave] who are brave and always like fighting; but there is no use in that, no need to speak for it. Follow what the whites tell you."

7. The next day they went, and a half-Yuma half-Mohave who spoke English, José, interpreted. The captain said: "You Mohave, I want you to stop fighting. That is why I am here: if you try to fight, I will forbid it. You think you know how to fight. Well, we also know how. But we don't: we want all people to be friendly. If a tribe is bad, we will go against them; but if they are good, we do not trouble them."[11]

8. Aratêve said: "Good. I am the man who talks of fighting.[12] I am the one who says to these Mohave: 'Stop! Don't run! Fight!' When we are to have war against anyone, I talk. I speak four times and make wind and dust so that no one can see

---

Posts, 1800-1916. Fort Yuma, Calif., USNA [hereinafter cited as 617]. Heintzelman's report of these affairs, dated July 15, 1853, is in 34 Congress 3 Session, Executive Document no. 75 (Washington, D.C., 1857), pp. 34 ff.

[9] Further restatement of the known.

[10] Yara tav (short for eecheyara tav, beautiful bird) as the Mohave gave it. He was a hereditary chief in Mohave Valley, of one of the Hutto-pah bands or groups there; of the Neolge Clan; and, from his speech below in the text, a kwanami, a man who specialized his life toward warfare, a "brave man." From his granddaughter, Tcatc, George Devereux learned that he was a shaman. See Lorraine Sherer, "Great Chieftains of the Mojave Indians," *Southern California Quarterly*, 68 (March, 1966), 1-35, and *The Clan System of the Fort Mojave Indians* (Los Angeles, 1965), for these understandings that she worked out along with the present-day Fort Mojave Indians and by their kindness using the small tribal archive, with other source materials. Her analysis of clan and chieftainship and naming usages is especially important because all these matters were poorly understood in the nineteenth century and not fully clarified in previous field work. The chieftainship, for instance, was not as sharply etched or powerful a role (among Mohave, Quechan, Walapai, or Yavapai) as once thought by the whites. For information on naming practices that fits with Sherer's patterns, see Leslie Spier, "Some Observations on Mohave Clans," *Southwestern Journal of Anthropology*, 9 (1953), 324-328, 335, and George Devereux, *Mohave Ethnopsychiatry and Suicide: the Psychiatric Knowledge and the Psychic Disturbances of an Indian Tribe*, Bureau of American Ethnology Bulletin 175 (Washington, D.C., 1963), esp. 6-7, 549-552.

[11] These speeches are of course given because they portray the native idea of what the white commandant said.

[12] Self-assertive boasting: I am a warrior and a person of authority, even though from now I shall be peaceful. I desist voluntarily, not from compulsion.

me.[13] It was given to me: I was born like that.[14] Sometimes, near the enemy, I make it rain, so that they all stay indoors. Then when it is daylight, we attack. I tell my people: 'Fight! Don't run away!' And we always drive the others before us. But now I am quitting. I will stop saying and doing that. I will not forget what you tell me. But these others here, they know nothing, except to fight. I want you to give them a paper so they will know and will stop thinking about fighting."[15]

9. The commandant answered: "Good. I will give them letters. Who is it that always wants to fight? How many are brave men?" [16] Aratêve pointed them out, and the captain said: "Good. I will give you letters, you five, to take home with you. If [white] people come to where you live show them the paper and they will know who you are and that you are a chief of your tribe. If you fight again, now that you have the letters, I will send soldiers to live in your land. But if you do not fight or steal horses or kill cows, everything will be well."

10. So they got their letters. They were all ranked evenly then; later on, some were intelligent and were ranked ahead and became chiefs. This was before there were any whites at Fort Mohave. They had no shirts or pants [with pockets] at that time; so the brave men, not knowing where else to put their letters, put them under their string belts.[17]

11. When they arrived home, I knew those that had got papers. They are all dead now.[18] They were Kapêtáme; Asikáhota;[19] Tapaikunehe; Hatsūr-ama, whose name, "cold-travel," meant that he would go to war even in winter; and Nyasaiyo-nyakiūve, who when he was a young man had the name Hatšur-īya, "mouth is cold." The last two were friends and partners.

12. And the captain saw the two women captives. "Take them along to your homes," he said.[20]

13. It took them ten days to get home from Yuma with the two prisoners. They

---

[13] The association of dust and war is repeated tiresomely by the Mohave, in myth, in song, in names, in the mourning commemoration. It is evidence of how near to the surface reality of risk of life in grim fighting is the reliance on supernatural power.

[14] Meaning that he dreamed of war—probably of hawks.

[15] He himself did not want a paper; as again, in Episode 3, below. Perhaps he was too great a man to need it. Or, he may have considered a letter a magical means to turn a warlike mind to peace, and he himself was already for peace.

[16] Kwanami, professional brave man, "warrior."

[17] The belt served chiefly to hold up the breech clout. This may have been braided or woven of cord in the old days; possibly the belt also, hence this mention of "string."

[18] Probably dead a long time in 1903, else Chooksa homar might have resisted naming them. In Episode 6, below, two of them are said to have been dead then, some years later.

[19] Homose-quahote (orator of the stars), hereditary chief of the northernmost (Matha lyathum) of three groupings of the Mohave, this one living from Black Canyon down to Piute Wash. From his family being of the clan Malika and he being elected from that clan, he was "Great Chieftain" of the nation, Aha macave pipatahon: see Sherer, "Great Chieftains," pp. 2-5 passim. He was a kwanami; and it has been asserted that kwanamis did nothing else but dream of and lead to war; but see Leslie Spier, *Mohave Culture Items* (Flagstaff, Ariz., 1955), who discusses possibilities of overformulation of Mohave war patterns. I feel that to ascribe exclusively war activity to the kwanami may be overformulation.

[20] It seems doubtful whether an army officer would knowingly authorize the carrying away of women prisoners. Possibly the narrator was still protecting his tribesmen against having committed a crime, in white American eyes, fifty years before [A.L.K.].

brought them to Qavkūaha,[21] a few miles downstream of Fort Mohave. So the
southern half of the tribe did not have slaves, the northern half did.[22] The whole
tribe came together at Qavkūaha to see the slaves: I was a boy and I was there.
They were going to give them to the Qohôta,[23] the man that always works, builds
a large house, feeds everybody, and makes dances for them. It was midafternoon
when they arrived at his house. Qohôta had sent two of his kinsmen with the war
party, to attend to captives if they took any. These two men carried water[24] for
the captives on the way, gave them food at night, and walked behind them.
When the women got too tired, they sat down, [and these men waited with
them.][25] So now they all came to Qavkūaha.

14. [Here the narrator gave an extended account of the celebration instituted
by the Qohôta, ending with the adoption of the captive girls as Mohave—really a
purification in the river.][26]

15. [After the celebration], Qohôta took the two Cocopa slaves to his house.
They were sisters, both called Orro.[27] This means night-hawk in Mohave, but in
Cocopa it is a woman's [clan] name. Now they saw no white people [in the
country as yet]; and about the five brave men fighters who had received letters at
Yuma, Qohôta said: "They will not fight any more; it is good."

16. Then he gave one of the slaves to an old man to marry, saying: "Only five
were fighters, but now they no longer want war. Perhaps these women will have
sons, half-Mohave half-Cocopa, and when they are grown up they will help keep
peace."[28] So she was married, and in two or three years she had a child.

17. But the other one was not married. Then Qohôta said: "There is no more
fighting. We had better send her home. There is no use keeping her if all [tribes]

---

[21] Qavkūaha was in Mohave Valley, east side, "several miles" below Fort Mohave (nine miles, as
seen in Episode 8, below) and is point I on map 1 (see back cover pocket) reproduced from A.L.
Kroeber, *A Mohave Historical Epic,* University of California Anthropological Records, 11:2 (Berkeley,
1951), where it is given as Qāv-kuraha and its location described on p. 139. This was on an island,
near its upper end.

[22] Prof. Sherer, "Great Chieftains," pp. 5, 29, explains that there was a tripartite division: Matha
Iyathum from Black Canyon to the head of the valley; Hutto-pah in the valley; and Kavi Iyathum
below The Needles. By 1859 there was one chief in the northern group (Homose-quahote), five in the
valley, and one (Ho-mar-rah-tav) well to the south. Sherer, p. 12, quotes the only statement I have
seen by a white man of the time that substantiates both regional groupings and chieftainships
together: Lt. Helenus Dodt's letter (as Indian Agent) of Aug. 23, 1870: "The tribe is divided in three
principal parts whose chiefs are Sickahut, Iritaba, and Aschuket, the former being the head chief of
the whole tribe. Each one of these parts is again divided into a number of hereditary captaincies." For
Asukit, see below.

[23] A.L.K. recorded also qwehota and qohot (or kwohota, kwohot). It is a title, not an individual's
name, and might be translated "fiesta chief." The Mohave specified the qohôta was not a hanidale,
that is, not a political chief (hanidale probably being a rendering of Spanish, *general*). Satilpotiya was
mentioned by Chooksa homar as a qohôta who died about ten yrs. before, i.e., about 1893; and he
may have been the last one (A.L.K.) Leslie Spier, *Yuman Tribes of the Gila River* (Chicago, 1933), p. 158,
wrote that this derivation of hanidhala "looks to me like folk-etymology on the part of the Mohave."

[24] Probably in stoppered gourds.

[25] They were treated with consideration, subject to not slowing the pace of the party. Tôkwaθa's
account, in "Olive Oatman's Return," shows that if they could not keep up with the men they were
allowed to reach camp later, under guard of course.

[26] A summary of this celebration is in A. L. Kroeber, *Handbook of the Indians of California*
(Washington, D.C., 1925), pp. 745-747.

[27] It is a Cocopa clan name, and no doubt signifies night hawk in that language also.

[28] As before, in sections 2 and 17.

are friends." So some men brought her to the Yuma, and there the Cocopa met her and took her home. And that was the time the soldiers called in the Cocopa and other tribes to tell them again to be peaceable.

18. The other sister is still alive [1903] on Parker Reservation, and is still called Orro. She had a son and a daughter. The girl died, but the man is living.

19. Qohôta said: "We have quit fighting: there is no use [opportunity] dancing in connection with that. So dance where you like, and when. If there still were war, I would summon you all. But there is no fighting, so I will call you no more."

EPISODE 2. FIRST CONFLICT WITH AMERICANS

20. After this it was about seven years that the whites came from the east with wagons and cattle, to [Hardyville crossing] about three miles above Fort Mohave.[1] I was then a boy about so high [point: ca. twelve years], living opposite Needles. I [went up river and] saw two white women and a boy, then two more with a child, and more coming behind. There was a man with them who had calico and was cutting off lengths and giving each Mohave man a piece, and a ring and two or three little bells: I saw that. Then they gave me about four feet of calico for a breechclout and a ring and a small bell.

21. By afternoon, all the whites had reached the river and drove the cattle down to where they would have grass at [the foot of where] Fort Mohave [was later]. All the Mohave stood on the mesa looking; [many of them] had not seen whites or horses [sic] or cattle before. They looked at the cattle but would not go near them, fearing to be hooked. In the evening they returned to where they slept, which was where some Mohave had their houses, near by.

22. Next morning, some of the head men said: "Do not go to the whites today." Aratêve was then at Yuma; but the five brave men who had been given letters were there and said: "I tell you: I want to fight the whites." Other Mohave said: "That paper you got does not tell you to fight. It says to be friendly to the whites: you brought it to our land from Yuma." They answered: "Oh well, I will tear it up. They just wrote on the paper, but that will not stop me, I did not want

---

[1] John Udell, *Journal Kept During a Trip Across the Plains* . . . . (Los Angeles, 1946: orig. publ. Jefferson, Mo., 1868); Leonard J. Rose, *L. J. Rose of Sunnyslope* (San Marino, Calif., 1959), pp. 3-21; Rose's long letter of Oct. 28, 1858, in R. G. Cleland, *The Cattle on a Thousand Hills: Southern California, 1850-1870* (San Marino, 1941), pp. 306-315, from *Missouri Republican* of Nov. 29, 1859; and ms. letter of twenty members of the emigrant party to Commandant, Fort Defiance, from Picacho, Sept. 22, 1858, Records of the War Department, Adjutant General's Office, B70/1 AGO 1858, USNA, and Major E. Backus's letters of Oct. 12 and 15 in the same file [this record group in the Archive hereinafter cited as AGO]; "Yesar" [Rasey Biven] in *San Francisco Alta California*, May 28, 1859; Commissioner of Indian Affairs A. B. Greenwood to Secretary of the Interior, Washington, D.C., Feb. 5, 1860, in Records of the Office of Indian Affairs, Report Books of the Bureau of Indian Affairs, 1838-1881, USNA. The *Los Angeles Star*, Nov. 13, 1859, copied the Sept. 22 letter; see the *Star* also for March 19, 1859. We thank Prof. Henry Dobyns for informing us of the "Yesar" letters and for sending us complete copies.

This first emigrant party to try the 35th-parallel route to California had accumulated eighteen wagons, more than two hundred people, about three hundred seventy-five cattle and about forty horses. The attack occurred Aug. 30, 1858. Probably nine whites were killed outright. The survivors took two wagons, about twenty cattle and about ten horses back toward Albuquerque, and survived because of meeting two other emigrant trains and because of the army's prompt and solicitous efforts on the trail and after the destitute people reached Albuquerque.

their paper; I did not ask for it, they gave it to me. I do not want the whites to come and own the land. They will take it and keep it. I want to stop them, to kill them all."

23. The other Mohave said to them: "Well, if you five want to fight, go fight. But we will not help you. If you think you can fight them [successfully], go ahead."[2]

24. The five answered: "If we let the whites come and live here, they will take your wives. They will put you to work. They will take your children and carry them away and sell them. They will do that until there are no Mohave here. That is why I want to stop them from coming, want them to stay in their own homes. The eastern Indians, I hear that is what the [whites] did to them there: they took their children and said to them: 'You are not to see your parents.' And they keep birds eggs and coyotes and bears and every kind: maybe they will keep you all [confined] in a place too. As for me, I do not want them to do that to me. The whites will not listen to the Mohave. If you tell them to do something, they say No."[3]

25. The old men spoke against the five. [Their arguments are omitted because they are a repetition about the papers: the letters do not say to fight, but to be friendly.]

26. The five answered: "The whites, when you come near them, push you away; they kick you. A woman, if she is kicked, cries. I am a man: I do not cry: I do not want to be kicked."[4]

27. In the afternoon, the other Mohave said: "I have heard that these whites are everywhere, on all sides. You have heard that too. Nevertheless you want to fight them. Well, we will follow your counsel: we will go to fight."[5]

28. "That is what we want. We are not like mountains: we do not stay forever. We are not like the sky, always there; not like the sun or the moon: we die. Perhaps in a year, in a month, in two or three days. I want to die fighting."[6]

29. "Well, how many times do you wish [expect] to die? You die once and do not come alive again. We will fight with you and die too. No one likes to die. If you like it, why not tie your hands and feet and jump into the river? No one does that way: that is killing oneself. So you say you want to die soon: well, good, we will go along and help you."[7]

30. So they all got their clubs and bows and painted and put on feathers.

---

[2] The argument shows how little organized control of tribal action did exist.

[3] The warriors may have been actuated by pride and need to maintain their repute, but their apprehensions were largely justified. Their pacifist elders probably sensed defeat if it came to a contest; but in their answer in the next paragraph they carefully do not avow this, but keep harping on the Yuma letters as if these were fetishes.

[4] We do not often get this consideration expressed in white-native relations, though it unquestionably was a factor in many cases (A.L.K.). For episodes of earliest white-Indian contact in which kicking was followed by deadly response by the Indians: Forbes, pp. 312-313 (John Glanton on the Colorado, 1850), and Daniel Conner, *Joseph Reddeford Walker and the Arizona Adventure*, ed. Donald J. Berthrong and Odessa Davenport (Norman, Okla., 1956), p. 111 (Joe Walker's party on the Hassayampa, 1863).

[5] The peace party begins to yield to nationalistic sentiment, but still with a current of bitterness, as in section 29.

[6] These are stock Mohave sentiments and phrases which we will encounter again.

[7] They are more prudent, but not ready to admit less bravery, so they agree to go along though suggesting it is mere suicidal folly.

When they became angry like this, they used to tie their hair tightly together at the nape,[8] letting the ends hang down loose. They painted the hair red, the face black;[9] that is how they liked to die.

31. The whites were camped about a mile away, at the river among the cottonwoods at the foot of Fort Mohave terrace, west of it. Now the five said: "Are you ready?" and when they were, they all went toward the whites, the five leading.

32. And they notified the Chemehuevi who were living in Nevada across the river from Fort Mohave. There was a Chemehuevi named Ahwetaraδme[10] who had said: "When you decide to fight, send word: I want to fight too."

33. But when they came nearer, some of the Mohave did not want to fight after all[11] and went up on the [Fort Mohave] mesa and stood there: they wanted to see it. Those who wanted to fight, a good many, went on with the five.

34. When they came within two or three hundred yards, the whites saw them, went into their canvas-covered wagons, and got their guns. They did not shoot but stood there looking: they thought the Mohave might be coming to shake hands. The Chemehuevi were approaching from the west, up the river bank, from behind the white camp. When they came close, the Mohave ran forward, to seize the whites; then these shot, and the Mohave shot arrows, and they fought there. And the Chemehuevi stood and shot arrows.[12]

35. Savêre,[13] the leader of the whites, had ridden downstream with one companion to look for a good place [to cross]. He did not see the fight start, but heard the shooting, and rode back, when he ran into the Chemehuevi. These recognized him as the leader and all shot at him. He was hit by four or five arrows, and though he reached his camp, he fell and died: the whites put him into a wagon.

36. "All right, you who say how many times you want to fight: we die once, but you also will die once only"—the Mohave, who had said that to the five brave men got shot in the breastbone and killed. One Mohave was hit in three places: the right ankle, above the right knee, in the left thigh. Another was shot through the right thigh. Still another was hit in the flank: the bullet stayed in.

37. When Savêre began to be struck by the arrows, the Mohave saw it and wanted to seize him and pull him off his horse.[14] One of them got under the horses and was running between them when Savêre's companion shot at him, but only tore the skin on his back.

---

[8] Probably to render it less easy for opponents to grasp. The cylinder-headed war club was made for an uppercut thrust into the face while the foe's head was being pulled forward by its long hair.

[9] Cf. A. L. Kroeber, *A Mohave Historical Epic,* paragraph 137 of the narrative, at p. 97.

[10] His Mohave name: "Foreign-taraδme."

[11] More disunity. The effect of guns was no doubt known by repute if not in the experience of the majority.

[12] It would seem that although these were nonwarlike emigrants, the guns sufficed to keep the Mohave from coming to hand-to-hand grip as their brave men prided themselves on doing. It is of interest that none of the five professional braves was among the casualties.

[13] Savedra in the records, an experienced guide whom the U.S. Army commander in New Mexico induced the party to take, before he recommended that they proceed—probably José M. Savedra (more likely correctly spelled as Saavedra). The wagon master was Alpha Brown.

[14] To club: the proper termination of combat, as in our old Infantry Manual it used to be by bayonet.

38. Two Mohave got two horses without being seen, during the fighting, and rode them off. One of them got a blue horse, the other a yellow with a stripe on its nose. I saw them do this.

39. So four Mohave were shot with bullets, one of them dead. They carried him and the wounded back to camp. The Chemehuevi jumped into the river and crossed back to the west side; also some Mohave who had come over with them. As these had been behind the whites, when the two lines of Indians shot with their bows and missed the whites, they could hit each other; and so the Mohave wounded in the thigh was shot by a Mohave.[15] When the dead man—his name was Tšapotire[16]—was brought in to his camp, everybody wailed.

40. All four of the wounded lived on the west side of the river. So all the Mohave crossed over there, leaving their effects on the Arizona side.

41. Then one man, Solī was his name, said, "I can cure those shot: I dreamed of powder, bullets, cartridges." So he treated them.[17]

42. That night they sent two men back to scout the whites. They crossed to the Arizona side and came near the camp. The whites were loading everything into their wagons, and then turned back on their way, back to the east, leaving their cattle.[18]

43. About daylight the two scouts returned. "Nobody is there, only cattle." Then the five fighters who had the letters said: "Well, we will all return to the other side, take the cattle, kill and eat them." Those of the Mohave who had come up from Needles and elsewhere downstream said: "We will not kill ours here, we will drive them home to eat." So they crossed that morning to take their cattle: I went with them. Some got two cows, some several: they drove them into the river to cross. If ten or twenty men lived in one place, they got several cattle: by afternoon, everybody had some and ate meat.

44. I had none for myself: I was too young, and afraid. But every day I went about the settlements and was given meat.

45. Now they thought that the whites had left for good.[19] The five fighters said: "You see, no more whites are coming. That is why I wanted to fight. If they had stayed in the country, they would never have left and would have taken everything: that is what I heard about them. Now we have fought and beaten them and they have gone back, far away; it is well, we own the land."

Episode 3. Peace Made with the Maricopa

46. At Yuma Aratêve learned of the Mohave fighting the whites. After three months he returned. He said: "I hear you fought, though I told you not to. And

---

[15] By an arrow. The others were hit by bullets.

[16] After a half century, the dead name taboo is weaker.

[17] Guns were known though not yet possessed; so someone promptly dreamed of them and had his cure ready.

[18] The Rose accounts show that the whites were in fear of their lives, deeply shocked by the unexpected hostilities; and in any case they had lost sight of the cattle and thought these had all been spirited off hours before.

[19] This incident tended to be recalled by whites whenever the Mohave name was mentioned. It was crucial in setting the white man's view of the tribe and it reverberated on in official circles because of

you will have war again: I know it. You used to fight the Maricopa. I want to go [to Phoenix] to see the Maricopa and tell them: 'The Mohave will not come any more to attack you.' "

47. Then he took five men and started ["for Phoenix"] southeast.[1] He sent one man to go directly to the Maricopa and tell their brave man Ahwan-tševarîh[2] at Avi-vave[3] that Aratêve was coming and would camp at Aha-kupînye, Agua Caliente,[4] and await the Maricopa there. There was no settlement then at Aha-kupînye, only the hot spring. He said: "If I do not send word in advance but go [directly] to where they live, they will think I have come to attack them."

48. The messenger, Amat-aqâqa,[5] [reached the Maricopa and] said [to Ahwan-tševarîh]: "Send some men to meet Aratêve." The Maricopa went on horseback and reached Agua Caliente about sundown.[6] They brought wheat bread and mesquite bean [meal] and the Mohave ate. In the morning they all started, the Mohave riding behind some of the Maricopa, and reached Avi-vave at sunset.

49. Aratêve shook hands[7] with Ahwan-tševarîh and said: "You are not coming to our country so we came to you. You know why. We did not come to take your belongings: it is for something else. We wish not to fight: that is why we came. If you say that too, I will hear it; but [in addition] I want you to take me to Sakatôna and Tusôn[8] where the whites live, and tell them my message. Tell them I say: 'I will fight no more. I will not change my mind; I want to stop fighting.' "

50. Ahwan-tševarîh said: "When you used to come to this land and made war, you got captives and took them away. What did you do with them?[9] Are they still alive? Did they sicken and die? Did you kill them?"

51. Aratêve said: "No, we did not kill them. When we got home, we gave her to an old man to marry. She had a daughter, and she[10] is married to a Mohave."

---

a claim entered against the U.S. government by some of the emigrants, for losses incurred here (see Greenwood's letter cited above, n. 1, Episode 2) (C.B.K.).

[1] He meant the place where Phoenix was later established.

[2] From the look and sound of this name, I assume it was Juan Chivaria as the whites styled him, leader in Maricopa war. His photograph appears as plate 5.

[3] Avi-'vave is the conspicuous, isolated Pima Butte about one mile east of Sacate, then the most southeastern Maricopa village called Misekwinily: Leslie Spier, *Yuman Tribes,* p. 20 and map 16, p. 21. On p. 23 Spier gives the name as Vivava (solitary mountain) [A.L.K.]. Specific Maricopa village locations are now under study again in the Department of Anthropology, the University of Arizona.

[4] North side of the Gila, far downstream, half way between Big Bend and Mohawk Mts. See Spier, *Yuman Tribes,* map, p. 19.

[5] "Raven-earth."

[6] Some riding: the airline distance by map is seventy-five miles.

[7] Probably learned from the whites.

[8] Sacatón and Tucson. That an officer "lived" there argues for a date in 1862 or 1863, when first Confederate States' and then U.S. Army traffic moved along the Gila Trail, sometimes involving stopovers at and near Sacatón. An army captain went to live at Sacatón upon retirement from the service in 1865.

[9] The captives are of first concern, at any rate the precondition to acceptance of good faith and further negotiation. C.B.K. assumes that form and content in this conversation may have been de rigueur, ritualistic or symbolic, and likewise its very use here by the narrator. But the two "brave men" could have been discussing real captives, not from the Mohave-Yuma attack on the Maricopa in 1857, which took no captives, but perhaps from similar encounters in 1833, 1842-1845, or 1850-51, depending somewhat upon whether "she" in the text means the captive or the captive's daughter.

[10] Ambiguous between mother and daughter.

Ahwan-tševarỉh said: "It is well: you did not kill them." He thought that if the Mohave had killed their captives, there would be more war. [Aratêve[11] said:] "If a captive has a boy, it is he that [may] want to come here to fight you. It is not the true Mohave, it is a cross-breed that wants to fight."[12]

52. The Maricopa chief said: "Now I know it: you say they are still living. I know their kin who are still alive here. When we make peace, I want the half-Maricopa-Mohave to live, half of them here, half in your country. Then we shall be like kin, friendly. That is what I wanted to know about."

53. They stayed there [at Avi-vave] three days. Then, in the morning they went east with Ahwan-tševarỉh, all on horses, and at sunset reached Sacatón, where there was a white captain of soldiers: there were no white people at Phoenix yet.[13]

54. Ahwan-tševarỉh took him to the [United States Army] officer and said: "He is a Mohave; he came to me about ending war, and wanted me to bring him here to the whites."

55. The officer said: "If a man who has liked fighting wants to stop, it is good. You Maricopa did not want war; it was the Mohave, and each year they came and jumped into your enclosures. Now they say they will quit, and that is good. It was right for you to kill them [formerly], because they attacked you without right. But this man knows better. It is good. I will write a paper and give it to him."

56. But Aratêve said: "No, I do not want a paper. Take my name and put it in your book and keep it always."[14]

57. From there they went to Tucson, which then had only five houses: Sacatón had one.[15] They spoke the same, and that commandant also wanted to give Aratêve a paper, but he refused.

58. Returning, they slept at Sacatón, and after being gone three days and nights they got back to Avi-vave.[16]

59. That night and the next they did not talk [in council]. After two days, at night, Aratêve spoke. "Everything is settled: there will be no more fighting. We will shake hands and say: kiyỉ, kiyỉ." That is a Maricopa kinship word.[17]

---

[11] This speech is not attributed to anyone, in my record (A.L.K.).

[12] Point not clear: usually captives were desired on the ground that their intertribal children made for peace, as seen in the next paragraph.

[13] The distance to Sacatón would be only about fifteen miles, too near for all-day horseback. It is becoming evident that Chooksa homar did not remember distances in the Maricopa country and simply estimated each stage of the journey to have taken a day (A.L.K.). The main issues I see relating to this incident concern its date, Yara tav's possible motives for making peace at that time, and whether or not all this occurred as given or is a distorted account of a known peace meeting at Fort Yuma in April, 1863. See Discussions, below (C.B.K.).

[14] He was probably not thinking of posterity but of his own lifetime. As to not wanting a paper to carry, see the first episode. Later we will see that, in a different time and place, Yara tav did have the paper, often.

[15] Sacatón probably had one adobe structure at that time, although Conner, *Walker,* p. 74, does not mention it when he passed by there in April 1863. Tucson was a sizeable settlement, but Yara tav may have visited the improvised U.S. Army camp on the outskirts.

[16] Tucson is seventy or more miles from Sacatón, so it is impossible to have ridden so arduously as to crowd the round trip and a formal session with the commandant into two days. This time Chooksa homar's passion for the exact place and duration is stronger than his knowledge or remembrance.

[17] Spier, *Yuman Tribes,* pp. 213-214, for Kiyỉ, man's term for most cousins of the same generation,

"Whenever I see a Maricopa, I will shake hands and say: Kiyī. Now we will shake hands, and tomorrow we will go home. When we arrive, I will tell my people what you [Ahwan-tševarīh] said. I will tell them all about it."

60. In the morning they wanted to give them food for the journey, cakes of ground wheat and mesquite,[18] and got it ready and gave it to them. Aratêve said: "That will last me for four days. When I am nearing home, this will be eaten up, but it is enough, I will go on [without food] until I arrive."

61. Toward noon Ahwan-tševarīh stood up and orated[19] to his assembled people. "In the mornings, a coyote would howl and scare you: 'It is the Mohave, war is coming' you thought, and seized your bows and clubs; now that is over. Some days, an owl would hoot in the morning—'look out, war is here,' you would say. Now there is no more fighting. Let coyote yelp: you can sleep. When we still fought, we all got up early, we were afraid to sleep late. Now we can sleep after the sun is up. If you see a Mohave anywhere, go to meet him; do not be afraid, shake hands, talk with him. Now my friend is leaving for home: let all shake hands with him. All go to him, shake his hand, say: kiyī; say what I say. You women, shake his hand too, say siyī.[20] Let the men shake first, then all the women." As they took hands, both spoke the word. A woman said siyī: to a man and he to her.

62. Aratêve said: "I said I was going. When I reach home, I will tell your relations, the half-Maricopa. They will want to come to see you. Perhaps they will bring you aqwêre red paint, perhaps amat-eh'ê white paint."

63. Then they went home. In about ten days[21] they reached [Mellen at] the foot of the Valley. Then he sent word to all Mohave settlements. "Tell them Aratêve went to a foreign tribe to stop war. He has come back, safe: the Maricopa did not kill him. He will tell everything; he wants all to know it. Aratêve lives at Aha-kwa-a'i;[22] in two days, in the morning, he wants all to come there; he will tell what he said to the Maricopa."[23]

64. In two days, everybody came. He told them the whole story. When he had finished, he said to the five fighting men: "I do not want you to do that [attacking the whites] again. Will you fight them next time, or what? I do not want it. If you do so again, I will somehow fix you."[24]

---

and "friend," term of greeting between non-related men, in Maricopa. See n. 20, Episode 3, below.

[18] Ahtšiêta moδile, "wheat head," metate-ground wheat, parched, in a loaf, eaten raw (dry). Aya-tšuvanve, a hard cake of pounded mesquite bean flour, broken and stirred into water, then drunk.

[19] This is a formal, rhetorical speech.

[20] Spier, *Yuman Tribes,* pp. 213-214, ciyi, i.e., shiyi, corresponding to kiyī; between women, or to an acquaintance of opposite sex.

[21] The ten is rounded. A place-by-place itinerary recorded elsewhere (*A Mohave Historical Epic,* pp. 146-147) from the same informant has a war party spending seven nights, eight days on the way.

[22] Heard as Aha-kwa-'īye, "directly opposite Needles, on the East edge of the Valley, a high place on a large lake or slough." It was recorded as Aha-kaw-'a'i, no. 28 east side on map 1, *A Mohave Historical Epic,* and is mentioned below in Episode 9, section 125; and as Aha-kwai in A. L. Kroeber, *Seven Mohave Myths,* University of California Anthropological Records, II:1 (Berkeley, 1948), Vinimulyepatše, p. 24. "Opposite" would probably mean northeast: it was probably not far from Aha-kukwiuve.

[23] Not only does he want an audience, but he will tell them what he said to others. These great leaders manifest some naive self-complacencies.

[24] "Fix" in the interpreter's colloquial English. The threat is surprising. "Block" or "prevent"

Episode 4. Second Conflict with Americans

65. It was two years later that white people came again. This time they came from the west. The Chemehuevi at Piute Spring, Aha-kuvílye, the stinking spring north of Ibex, saw them on the way and sent word to the Mohave. The whole tribe heard it and saw them coming raising the dust, and gathered to see them [where they were heading for] at Aha-kw-aΘo'ilye,[1] the long salty lake half a mile from the river, across from Fort Mohave. All wanted to meet them; the five wanted to fight again.

66. Then Aratêve called out: "Come here, if you want no fighting! Let those fight who like it!" So, many came over to him, but fewer went to the five [warlike men]; and these started to meet the whites.

67. However, they did not attack, but met the Americans and went along with them. There were eight wagons, plus some riding horses. Now they had reached Aha-kw-aΘo'ilye and were unharnessing: the Mohave stood all around them. The head of the whites was handing out tobacco. The Mohave were painted and feathered and had clubs and bows: it looked like there would be fighting. The whites knew it too, and dug a ditch, deep to half-way the thigh, and started to sit in it with their guns. That was all that happened that day. At night the Mohave drew off about two miles down river. Aratêve [had] kept saying: "Keep back! Go back! The whites are afraid of you."

68. In the morning the Mohave sent a man up to scout. He reported: "The whites are moving eastward. They have started [from their camp] for the river." All went to see: "Yes, they are going east." At the river the whites fixed up two [pontoons] to cross with, large tents filled with air. Two of them went on top of these to try the crossing. All the Mohave stood there watching: I saw it too.

69. When they saw that [the pontoons] would float all right, they started to turn back in the middle of the river. Thereupon the Mohave lined up on the east bank began to play with them: they shot close past them. They were not wanting to hit them and missed deliberately, but near by. When the two on the floats returned, they said: "Those on the far side are mean." "Yes, we saw it," the others said. So they gathered their effects, hitched up, and went back to their camp at Aha-kw-aΘo'ilye, giving up the crossing.

---

would be less personally minatory: but there may be no such Mohave word. In addition, there probably was no mechanism in the society for actually preventing anyone, except by the dangerous way of threat or force. There is some play for power evident. Aratêve wants to stand well with the whites, comes out for peace, and has the whites try to restrain the five professional brave men. In his absence they involve part of the tribe in an attack on the whites, and all of them in cattle stealing. His trip to the Maricopa is an obvious endeavor both to repair his home prestige and to resolidify himself with the whites (A.L.K.).

[1] Beaver Lake: it was used later as a camping place, by whites (A.L.K.). The thirty-eight men, ten camels, and six wagons with their six-mule teams left Los Angeles March 1, led by S. A. Bishop whose objective was to meet and supply the expedition of Lt. Edward F. Beale (approaching the Colorado River from the east, marking out the best wagon route): see Bishop to Major Hoffman, Pah-Ute Creek, March 24, 1859, and W. W. Hudson to Col. Warner, written not before April; copies in Huntington Library, San Marino, Calif., from Hayes Collection, Bancroft Library, University of California, Berkeley; printed in *Southern Vineyard,* May 3, 1859; see issues also of April 22 and 29, and *Los Angeles Star,* April 16, 1859.

70. Aratêve went where [he was having] beans[2] cooked for all the tribe and called: "Come, all of you, eat this! Don't follow the white men! Don't go near them! If you want to look at them, that is all right; but don't do more! If they see you are without clubs and bows, it will be well. If they see you carrying [weapons] and following them, there will be trouble." Aratêve then went off to a house.

71. But the five followed the whites; and, returned to Aha-kw-aΘo'ilye, they stood about 200 yards from them. Then the whites fired. I think they were angry at the arrows shot at the two on the river. I was there and saw it: I was about so high [pointing—perhaps age 14].

72. Then some Mohave shouted: "That's what you have been wanting! You like them to shoot at you."[3] A good many were carrying clubs and bows and were painted, as usual, though they were not meaning to fight. Some of these went off, to avoid [being involved.][4]

73. But the five brave men, along with some others, charged[5] the whites. One Mohave was shot in the side of his chest and killed: Haiqo-tšanalye, "White-man-lost," was his name.[6] And another, Ampote-kivauve, "Dust-stand-on," was shot in the arm. He was called that because as a boy he used to follow dust-whirlwinds in play and stand on them.[7]

74. The dead man was carried down [river] a short distance to where some houses stood, and wood was got, and he was cremated.

75. When the whites saw the fire, they started to turn back west and went off.

EPISODE 5. THE FIRST SOLDIERS ARRIVE

76. A year later, the whites came again from the west, at night: no one knew it, but there they were at Aha-kw-aΘo'ilye. Men out hunting[1] saw them, and a man was sent as messenger down each side of the river. These whites were soldiers, all cavalry, and they came ready for war. There were only about thirty of them, but no one went near them because they had guns, bayonets, and swords.[2] By afternoon many Mohave had collected, but they remained at the settlements.

---

[2] As usual, when a kind of food is specified it is *not* maize.

[3] Viz. "Now you have what you did to bring on." There are many more outbreaks of this naive, I-told-you-so irony in the sections that follow.

[4] There was neither discipline nor coercion in such situations. The peace party stayed away, the unsure came armed but prudently moved away when firing began and the bellicose attacked. It was only a surge of emotion that could make the tribe act as a unit.

[5] "Ran at them."

[6] Names were taken sometimes randomly or trivially, often with allusion to a unique experience or novel report. See n. 4, Episode 6.

[7] This would mark him out as a future warrior, dust being a symbol for war.

[1] Hunting is not often mentioned. Here they may have gone after rabbits or birds with curved throwing clubs.

[2] Even the professional braves seem to have been overawed. See Major William Hoffman's report of this reconnaissance (which was preliminary to establishing a post among the Mohave), Grass Valley, Calif., Jan. 16, 1859, *Report of the Secretary of War, 1859* (Washington, D.C. 1859), pp. 389-392, and in the same volume, his Jan. 19 letter and Jan. 27 report; and, by the two frontiersmen who acted as scouts on this trip, William E. Goodyear's longish letter in John S. C. Abbott, *Christopher Carson . . .* (New York, 1873), pp. 315-321; and Joseph R. Walker's brief conversation reported in *Southern*

77. Aratêve said to the five: "I told you not to fight them. If you did fight them, the soldiers would come, I told you. See, now they have come.[3] I knew that: you did not know that. Don't go to them: stay here! If they attack during the night, I will let you fight.[4] But don't go to meet them; stay in your houses; only if they shoot, then fight!"

78 Next day, when the sun was about half-way up, Aratêve said: "Well, let us go and stand up. If they want us, they will wave their arms. That will mean they want to shake hands."[5] Then they stood about one hundred yards from the soldiers, who were all mounted and drawn up.

79. Aratêve said: "I want two men to go forward,[6] close to each other. If the whites do not want war, [you will be able to] go on up to the captain. If they want to fight and shoot, jump apart and let the bullet go between you."[7]

80. So two men approached. Then a first sergeant shot, but they leaped apart and were not hit. Then all the soldiers fired, and hit three men, but killed none of them. One was struck in the knee, one in the upper thigh, a third through the lobe of his ear and in the temple. Then the soldiers all went off west again.[8] I saw them.

EPISODE 6. THE SOLDIERS ARRIVE IN FORCE

81. Then, when the wheat was ripe,[1] a messenger came from the Yuma to Aratêve. "When you were here, five of you received letters and said you would not fight any longer. But you still are fighting. You killed white people coming from the east and from the west. Now you can see soldiers gathering at Yuma from everywhere and starting up river against you. Some are coming walking, some on a steamboat. They have the Yuma chief Paskwāole[2] with them and he has a Kamia to interpret in English."[3]

Vineyard, Jan. 23, 1859 (transcript in Huntington Library). See also *Tubac Weekly Arizonian,* May 17, 1859. The encounter occurred January 7-9. The U.S. troopers were commanded by Lt. A. B. Chapman, 1st Dragoons.

[3] There is no end of such statements of vindication, both in the historical and in the mythical accounts.

[4] "Let you fight" implies his approval, not his permission: he had no more than suasive control.

[5] The brave men not being in evidence in the face of the soldiery, Aratêve apparently decided to try a friendly gesture.

[6] The soldiers not waving their arms as the emigrants presumably had done, Aratêve goes a step farther and asks for volunteer messengers.

[7] This naive safeguard, although it happened to work, is probably based on arrow-dodging.

[8] After the Mohave had immediately run off, no doubt. The whole incident seemed to the Indians unmotivated (A.L.K.). Hoffman was trying to establish (1) whether a Colorado River post could in fact be supplied directly overland from San Bernardino, and (2) where to put such a post along the west bank of the river. In the face of such determined opposition of incalculable strength, he withdrew, carefully stepping water supplies along with his small unit so as not to lose animals or men on the long trip back to the white settlements.

[1] That crop would ripen in about late April, in the valley, or in May; and the second crop, much larger, was planted after the river's overflow, thus about mid-June (corn, pumpkins, beans, melons): see Peter R. Brady, post interpreter, to Major G. O. Haller, commanding Fort Mojave, Oct. 9, 1860; Records of the War Department, U.S. Continental Army Commands, Fort Mohave, USNA [hereinafter, papers from this fund are cited as from 393].

[2] José María, a Yuma chief and often a translator, also came.

[3] The river Kamia were in one sense only western Diegueño who lived more or less permanently on

82. This interpreter's name was Hoalye-ime, "My leg is of yellow pine"; he called himself that when he saw a white man with a peg-leg.[4] The Kamia language is different from the Yuma, but some of them understood each other through living close together and associating; as the Mohave and Walapai have learned to understand each other.[5]

83. Now the foot soldiers, carrying blankets and guns, could not walk fast. They would go a way and make camp. Then the steamer would arrive, land, cook for them. So it took them about ten[6] days from Yuma to Mohave Valley. There were many soldiers: the upper and lower deck were full of them and more on foot. So they arrived at the foot of Fort Mohave terrace, where the Mohave had fought the whites that first came from the east. They had tents and made benches and little shades of willows there.

84. Captain Bôt[7] sent word around: "I want to see every Indian, the whole tribe." So they all came and camped near the fort,[8] and in the morning started to go to him, when the interpreter met them and said: "Captain Bôt wants you to carry no clubs or bows." So [some] gave their weapons to others [and went on], but those holding weapons went up on the mesa, [ready] to run in, if fighting began, and hand the bows back to their owners. I was one of those standing above; but all the old and head Indians went into the ramada. Captain Bôt knew from the Yuma who the five head men[9] were; two of them were dead by now; the three others sat on a bench.

the New River slough and, when this dried up, sometimes on the Colorado. Some of the Diegueño had probably already learned English (A.L.K.). [Forbes shows that Pascual himself probably was born and spent his childhood at New River (C.B.K.).]

[4] Illustrating the generalization made in n. 6, Episode 4. He was impressed by the sight, probably humorously; so he named himself for it (A.L.K.). See Sherer, *The Clan System,* pp. 11-23, for the first complete and reasonable explanation of naming practices among the Mohave. She shows that this kind of name was taken upon occasion (pp. 19, 23) but is able to relate the whole series of name customs back to the religious basis of the society.

[5] The linguistic classifications are correct: See A. L. Kroeber, *Classification of the Yuman Languages,* University of California Publications in Linguistics, 1 (1943), 21-40.

[6] An advance party of eighty men left Fort Yuma Feb. 8, 1859, to establish a supply depot about seventy-five miles upstream (Fort Gaston as it was called, then and later): Fort Yuma return, Feb. 1859, in 617. The main expedition, seven companies of infantry and two of artillery, left the fort in the last days of March and finally encamped near Beale's Crossing of the Colorado on April 19: Peter R. Brady, in *War of the Rebellion,* ser. I, vol. 50 (Washington, D.C., 1894), 911-912. See *Southern Vineyard,* Feb. 22, 1859; "Yesar" in *Sacramento Union,* March 2, 1859; Guard Reports, 6th Infantry, Dec. 1858-1859, AGO. Some of these events are reflected in *Report of the Secretary of War, 1859,* pp. 387-422 [hereinafter published annual reports are shown as *Report, War,* and so on].

[7] Capt. Henry Stanton Burton, ranking as captain in the 3rd Artillery from Sept. 22, 1847. He spoke for Hoffman during the meeting, to a Yuma, who spoke to a Mohave who had lived at Yuma, who spoke to the Mohave chiefs: E. Bandel, *Frontier Life in the Army, 1854-1861,* ed. Ralph P. Bieber (Glendale, California, 1932), p. 272.

[8] Sherer, "Great Chieftains," pp. 3-4 discusses the meeting and quotes brief paragraphs from the account left by Gwegwi nuor who was present, and so dictated his memoir in 1935: his account, brief as it is, accords in making Homose-quahote the spokesman for the Mohave.

The meeting convened on April 23: see Hoffman's view of the events discussed in the text, in his letter of May 18, 1859, *Report, War, 1859,* pp. 411-413.

[9] The five brave men of the first episode, or however many of them still were living, appear here. Aratêve is not included, and stands by the bench, although he had previously talked like a head chief. It sounds almost as if there might have been five recognized chieftainships with the incumbents thereof expected to show that they were brave—and, that Aratêve had never held one of them

85. With them sat two others, chiefs: Avi-havasūts, "Blue-rock," and Qolhoqorāu, a young man, Aratêve's nephew[10]—he died only recently. These two were against fighting. Next to them, at the end of the bench, stood Aratêve.[11] The three [survivors of the original five] brave men had to talk,[12] especially Asikahôta who always had been most insistent on fighting. His home was across the river from Fort Mohave in what is now Nevada; one of the two others lived far down Mohave Valley. Soldiers stood all around, and cannon were loaded.

86. I was up on the mesa, watching. Two men there wanted to go down to hear, so I went with them.[13] At first the soldiers would not let us in, but the chiefs called for us, so we were admitted. I stood there and heard Asikahôta talking to Captain Bôt. The five chiefs sat facing a cannon, with four soldiers by it, and five sergeants and corporals behind them. There were several benches, with Indians sitting all along them. Some had short clubs [concealed] under their belts, or stones and the like. The Indians had said, because there was a stockade all around: "If they begin to fight, don't try to run: we can't escape and they can't; just seize them immediately!"[14]

87. Bôt asked Asikahôta: "When you were at Yuma you got a letter, but after you returned home you continued to fight. Why did you do that?" Asikahôta said: "That's my way. I always fight. I like it."[15] Bôt asked: "Do all of these men like to fight and die?" "No, not all of them. They came to help me because I want them to. They do not like dying. It is I who want to die."[16] The interpreter said: "If you like to die, perhaps you will soon start to fight." "All right. If there is to be fighting, it is good with me. That is what I have been saying to you."[17]

88. Finally, Captain Bôt said: "Good. I hear what you say. But you are not fighting now. Well, I am returning [to Yuma]. I am leaving this lieutenant here to watch you. If you do anything wrong, he will kill you. And now, when I return, I want to take ten men along with me. I want you among them."

(A.L.K.). Prof. Sherer's published findings, cit. supra, strongly indicate seven hereditary chieftainships; and Peter R. Brady's report of Oct. 9, 1860, cit. supra, names the persons holding those positions in 1860.

[10] But here, and in nn. 24, 25, Episode 6, below, Aratêve's close kin are conspicuous, so that one gets the idea that if he is not among "the five" it is because he is big enough in repute and influence to exclude himself from them.

[11] The six chiefs facing Hoffman were the four just named in the narrative above, with two of the "brave men" who had received papers at Fort Yuma (Kapêtāme and Tapaikunehe), both now chiefs living on the west side of the river, in Mohave Valley. Peter Brady's report, cit. supra, shows that not two, but only one, of the Yuma five had died by this time (Nsaiye-ny-kūive); the other one simply did not come to this conference (Kapêtāme, or Koppatam, chief in the northern section of the valley, east of the river). All this squares with what Prof. Sherer has learned in recent years: that there were six chieftainships in the north, and one in the south (held by Ho-mar-rah-tav who was not involved in any of these hostilities or peacemakings).

[12] Were cross-examined.

[13] After all, he was still a boy or incipient youth.

[14] This is reminiscent of the Wounded Knee massacre, except that the Dakota do seem to have struck the first blow, and the Mohave were overawed and did not strike at all. But if it had come to a struggle, the close-up seizing was what they prided themselves for and relied on in battle.

[15] Curt, self-sufficient, almost truculent. The professional brave man verges on the defiant bully here, when cornered.

[16] Here he sets himself up above his following: "they are really afraid but my personality holds them in line." The implication is that his personality is superior because he is ready ("likes") to die. This readiness is the incessant refrain both of the professional braves and of those who reproach them.

[17] Take it or leave it.

89. Asikahôta said: "I will not be arrested. I like to die: I will not be taken. I am not going."[18]

90. Then Avi-havasūts said to him: "Now you are afraid. You keep saying you like to die; you would not listen to us but fought. Now, why don't you go with him? You are afraid to.[19] Well, if you're afraid, I'll go [instead]."[20]

91. And Qolhoqorāu said to him: "Yes, you make trouble and get arrested and then you are afraid and don't want to go along. Well, I will go. Let them arrest me."

92. Avi-havasūts said again: "They want ten men. Whoever wants to, let him say: 'I'll go.' These three brave men[21] want to stay home. I will let[22] them stay."

93. Tôkwaϴa, Musk-melon,[23] was a young man then and said: "I'll go." And Atsyôra-pūke said: "I go." Aratêve's son Tekse-ϴume was only a boy but said: "They arrest my cousin:[24] I will go with him." And Aspamekelyeho, Eagle-claws, Aratêve's other nephew, [volunteered].[25] Itšere-'itse said: "I will go too"; he was a relative of Inyo-kutavêre.[26] Ilyhanapau said: "I will go." And Tinyam-isalye, Hand-dark, said: "I too." That made nine.

94. Avi-havasūts said: "All the rest are afraid. There are eight besides me: now take us: we are nine. You wanted ten, but they are afraid."

95. The captain said: "Good. Nine will be enough. Take them to the steam boat." It was late afternoon and all the Mohave went to their houses. Some arrived home in a little while, some only around midnight.[27]

96. The next day they took the nine men on their way to Fort Yuma.[28] There they put them into jail. Yuma who came to the Mohave reported that they were there. The Mohave asked: "What will they do to them? Hang them up?" "No," said the Yuma, "just keep them and feed them."[29]

---

[18] This defiance of Homose-quahote is commented on in Discussions, below (C.B.K.).

[19] Here is the obverse, uttered by the prudent, peace-preferring leader: "You are afraid"—undoubtedly true, and yet not true also. He penetrates but cannot shake the bravado.

[20] And here he clinches his case: "I will do what you fear to do." Again the ultimate appeal is to courage. The policies are opposite, the values the same. He was volunteering to undergo imprisonment, perhaps hanging, as we see at the very end of this episode. A masochistic ingredient is again evident. The original motivation may have been reasoned prudence in the face of perceived white superiority, as it was vainglory on the opposite side: but in crisis the moral values were the same.

[21] This surely is biting irony. While it did not swerve the bravery party, it shows the strength of feeling among the pacifists.

[22] "I will let"—at least in the interpreter's rendering, where we would say "Let them!" Mohave evidently tends to use "I" for "we" in many situations.

[23] Narrator of "Olive Oatman's Return," and of the Origin of War myth, no. 16 in *More Mohave Myths*, University of California Anthropological Records, 27 (Berkeley, 1972).

[24] Qolho qorau, Aratêve's nephew.

[25] Making three from this one family.

[26] This is the man who, nearly fifty years later when he was blind, told me the "Great Tale" or Migration Epic published as VIII in "Seven Mohave Myths."

[27] If they came from the lower valley, it could be twenty-five miles home.

[28] On the California side, like the Indian Reservation, whereas Yuma city is in Arizona (A.L.K.). Major Hoffman was under orders to take hostages, unless indeed the Indians should fight him openly first: see Brig. Gen. N. S. Clarke to Hoffman, San Francisco, Jan 31, 1859, in *Report, War, 1859*, pp. 407-409. How the ten specified by Hoffman became nine is dealt with in Discussions, below. Hoffman himself left for Fort Yuma with most of the troops, beginning on April 26: see "Yesar" letter of April 28 in *Alta California*, June 11, 1859.

[29] The Yuma knew by experience, but the procedure was new and probably rather incomprehensible to the Mohave.

EPISODE 7. PEACEFUL RELATIONS WITH THE MILITARY

97. The soldiers staying at Fort Mohave cut trees and took the lumber up on the terrace to build barracks.[1] They hired Mohave to work for them and paid them with food. They had no fresh meat, only bacon, and this the Indians would not eat.[2] When the soldiers gave [3] them loaves of bread, they threw them into the river, not knowing [4] they were good to eat. For working all day, they would be given a cupful of wheat flour; this they took home, boiled part into a mush and ate it unbaked; the rest they would stir into water, then salt and drink it.[5] Or, instead of money they would pay them with coats or blouses. These the Mohave would tear into strips for breechclouts, or "sew"[6] several together into a blanket.

98. They worked at these buildings about a month. If they were paid money, they refused it.[7] Given cloth, they took it, or a knife they took, thinking it would be good for making bows and digging-sticks.[8] When the buildings were finished, the soldiers came up from the bottom near the river and lived in them; some of the officers were in tents.

99. A Yuma called Ahan-kuta'ère, who kept a store and also spoke "Mexican,"[9] came to stay at Fort Mohave; and a white man, Umpère, who kept a store and also spoke Mexican, interpreted between Ahan-kuta'ère and the officers. This Yuma told the Mohave what money was good for, but they still did not take it. Only after about a year, when the Mohave brought melons and soldiers gave fifty cents apiece for them,[10] did the Indians learn to know about money and no longer wanted old knives and clothes.

100. After a year, also,[11] the soldiers built a palisade of cottonwoods at Fort Mohave and covered it with mud. The Mohave worked at this, but not steadily, two or three days, or four or five.[12] Then they quit and took their pay and played hoop-and-poles with the money. They would bet ten dollars on two or three games. [If they won], they would not buy clothes, they would buy a horse.

101. A Mohave who had gone to Yuma as a boy now returned; so they had an interpreter. He was Ampote-pûke, Dust-pûke, also called Charlie Potepook.

---

[1] They built huts (*jacales*) for the one-hundred sixty-five men on the post: Armistead's letter of June 14, 1859, Letters Received, 1822-1860, AGO; and Fort Mohave return for May, 1859, in 617.

[2] They objected to the smoking and salting, perhaps, rather than to its being pork or greasy.

[3] The quartermaster, I assume.

[4] More likely it was the Mohave fear of eating other people's strange foods.

[5] A native pattern.

[6] Braid or weave? Nothing is known of Mohave sewing or awls (they did not make coiled baskets); and they could hardly yet have had steel needles.

[7] Having nothing much they knew to do with it. A store is mentioned in the next paragraph; but it probably catered at first only to the soldiers (A.L.K.). There was a sutler there from the first.

[8] Digging sticks are not often mentioned.

[9] This would be Spanish. The two Yuma chiefs (Pascual and José María) did not speak it, Chooksa homar added.

[10] This would be individual soldiers, I take it, not the quartermaster.

[11] The same year as mentioned in the last paragraph, presumably—not an additional one. One would expect the palisade would be the first construction by the little garrison left when the main force had departed. But perhaps there was not enough time: the parley and surrender occurred in April, the jailbreak in June, the open fighting in August 1859 (A.L.K.).

[12] As in later times, also. Sherer, *The Clan System,* reproduces a photograph of buildings at the fort in 1871, and explains that these were made of cottonwood poles and adobe.

102. The steamboat was coming up to the fort every month.[13] The Mohave did nobody any harm and stole nothing;[14] the Walapai did not come around but stayed at their homes in the east. But the Mohave would all go to the fort [from time to time], stay two or three days, then go back to their homes.

EPISODE 8. THE CAPTIVE MOHAVE ESCAPE

103. The Mohave at Yuma now had stayed in jail about a year: it was summer, perhaps in July, and the mesquite beans were ripe.[1] Then TôkwaΘa[2], one of the nine [hostages], said: "I thought they would keep me two or three months, perhaps a year. Now a year is over, perhaps they will keep me all my life. I want to run off." Some of the others agreed; TôkwaΘa kept urging.

104. The head of the nine, Avi-havasūts, said: "Well, when you run off, I will not. I could run but I won't.[3] So you will leave me. But if you want to flee, do so."[4]

105. Every day TôkwaΘa would say: "You know the time to escape: at noon, when they go to dinner, that is when we will break away. Some of you, if you aren't good runners, head that way, to the river, and jump in. We others, good runners, will head that way [south?]." So they agreed.

106. Now at noon they started, when the guard with a gun had his back turned. He saw them and shot; the soldiers [in the mess] stopped eating and ran to take their rifles. One of the soldiers tried to seize Avi-havasūts, who had not fled but was indoors, and took hold of him. One other Mohave who had not run[5] was there and seized the soldier's gun. He did not know how to shoot it, but it went off, and the soldier was shot. Then the mass of the soldiers came running and attacked the two Mohave and killed them. That is why the seven escaped without being hit.[6]

107. They all jumped into the Colorado river and swam downstream. The soldiers took a rowboat and went in pursuit. They caught up, but had left their guns,[7] and the Mohave took hold of their oar blades so the soldiers were afraid of

---

[13] Early river navigation, long since discontinued, though I still saw a stern-wheeler at Needles (A.L.K.). For a careful study of the early steamboating, see Arthur Woodward, *Feud on the Colorado* (Los Angeles, 1955).

[14] This is the character given them by several whites at the time, starting with Major Armistead.

[1] The hostages gave themselves up April 26 and were sent to Fort Yuma that day on one of the steamers. They had arrived at the fort on May 4: see "Yesar," in *Alta California,* June 11, 1859, and Fort Yuma return for May, 1859, in 617.

[2] This is the young man who in his old age narrated myth 16 (in A. L. Kroeber, *More Mohave Myths*) and the narrative in Kroeber, "Olive Oatman's Return."

[3] From pride, or perhaps out of consideration for Aratêve's peace faction. He was not too old to be a reasonably good runner. He was known to the whites at Cairook (Keruk), having been helpful and friendly to both Whipple's and Ives's expeditions in 1854 and 1858.

[4] Again illustrating the anarchic individualism of the Mohave.

[5] Unfortunately his name was not asked. If he had been one of the three near kinsmen of Aratêve among the hostages, the fact probably would have been mentioned. These three were TekseΘume, his young son; Aspa-mekelyeho (eagle claws), his nephew; and his other nephew Qolho qorau, already recognized as chief then and surviving until shortly before 1903.

[6] The breakout of hostages occurred in late June. It is mentioned in Gen. Clarke's letter, San Francisco, June 30, 1859, 393; and in Armistead's letter of July 3, 1859, in *Report, War, 1859,* p. 414. The whites erroneously thought they had killed all those who had been hostages.

[7] Perhaps dropping them on shore to seize oars.

being capsized: the current was swift there. If the soldiers seized an Indian by his hair, the Indian would grab his arm and pull down, nearly drag him overboard, until the soldier let go.[8] A white civilian in Arizona saw them going by this way and did nothing but look on; he did not shoot.

108. Three of the seven Mohave reached the Arizona [eastern or southern] bank. The civilian saw them but only watched. The three ran until they reached bushes, then continued upriver, seeking the thickest brush.

109. Four of the seven came to land on the California bank; mounted soldiers pursued them and shot but missed them. Only Tôkwaθa was wounded, and the ball stuck fast above the temple.

110. Now when these four got to where Yēke was living then,[9] the country was level and open, without any brush, and there were a good many whites there; but they only watched the pursuit.[10] Many soldiers had arrived by now, [some] mounted, and the Mohave had to leap into the river again. They were naked, because when they escaped they had shed their clothes. There were boats here too and some of the soldiers took them, and this time they kept their guns. So now they shot, but the Mohave dived (ho'opk) like ducks and were not hit. So they went way down river; then the soldiers gave up and let them go.

111. The four Mohave climbed out on the Arizona side, and the Yuma came to hide them in their houses, and kept them the rest of that day and over night. "They won't chase you any farther," they said.[11] Next morning they fed them and gave them shirts, and the four Mohave started for home, crossing the river back to the California side.[12]

112. Meanwhile the three who had first escaped to the Arizona side [were on their way and after some days][13] reached [the vicinity of] Parker. There they found Mohave, some of whom had been living there, off and on, more and more since the Mohave had taken the country away from the Halchidhoma.[14] There were Yuma there too, at times, for it was a rich country, with much game.[15] The

---

[8] Not only are the Mohave large-bodied and strong, but they are excellent swimmers, crossing and recrossing the river on slight provocation all their lives.

[9] He lived in the vicinity for many years as a ferryman: see B. A. Stephens, "A Biographical Sketch of L. J. F. Jaeger," *Quarterly Publication of the Historical Society of Southern California*, I (1888-1889). The best treatment is by Janet Lee Hargett, *Louis John Frederick Jaeger . . .* (M.A. thesis, Univ. of Arizona, 1967).

[10] As two paragraphs before. Perhaps the civilians looked upon it as a sporting event, or they already then had the American civilian disdain for professional enlisted soldiers. At any rate, they obviously had nothing to fear from a few unarmed Indians trying to run away, so they could be impartial.

[11] Quite sound psychology, in a case like this: for white Americans the race was over.

[12] This would be familiar to some of them, because the usual route from the Mohave to the Yuma left the Colorado near Picacho, a day's journey or so above Yuma, to cut inland along the chord of the east-bowing arc which the river makes in that latitude.

[13] About three days: see n. 16, Episode 8, below. This is fast travel. The party returning the Oatman captive used six-and-a-half days from Parker to Fort Yuma. Parker is two to three days below Mohave Valley, and the whole trip to Yuma is ordinarily spoken of as a ten-day one, in round numbers as above.

[14] About thirty years before. Spier, *Yuman Tribes*, p. 14, calculates that the Halchidhoma left the Colorado around 1825-1830—1828 has since been generally assumed as the date—and the events being described took place in 1859 (A.L.K.).

[15] The Mohave in general speak so little of hunting deer or even rabbits that the reference may be

resident Mohave asked: "Are there only you three left alive?" "We don't know. Let's wait. If any others got away, they may arrive tomorrow." And indeed, the next day the four others came. So now all who had escaped were together at Parker: two had been killed in the jail: that is why there were only seven here.

113. In the morning they started north and in about two days reached Mohave Valley: it was about five days since they left Fort Yuma.[16]

114. The Mohave in the valley passed around word that in three days they would have a [warriors'] commemoration [for Avi-havasūts and his companion]: Nyimi-tš-ivauk, cry-put, is what it is called, or Hipatšk for the running back and forth.[17] It was to be held at Qavkŭaha,[18] nine miles[19] below Fort Mohave. So they held it there, all one day and night.

EPISODE 9. OPEN WAR WITH THE AMERICAN TROOPS

115. Five days after the mourning commemoration, the five [sic[1]] that had been given letters began to say: "I thought the soldiers would do good things for us, but here they kill us at Yuma. We had better fight the whites."[2]

116. The kin of the two men killed [at Yuma] said: "You want to fight and die, you say. Well, if you die, we will die too. Every one of us will be killed."[3]

117. So together they started for Fort Mohave. The rest of the tribe went along to look on, not believing they would really fight.[4]

118. At Kuyak-akwāΘe,[5] below Fort Mohave, a white man was herding horses and mules. They killed him[6] and drove all the animals downriver to Aha-kevāra.[7] All the Mohave from the lower valley came there during the day and got horses.

---

to quail, waterbirds, or even wood rats (A.L.K.). Brady's report, cit. supra, says that "There is no game whatever in their country and they know nothing of the chase."

[16] They broke out at noon. They could hardly have reached Parker before the afternoon or evening of the third day thereafter. Then they waited a day for the others. So three-and-a-half plus one plus two makes six-and-a-half days elapsed, but "about five" spent in travel would be right enough.

[17] The Mohave used to call it "Annual" in English, but it was held soon after death, as here, not a year later, nor at any fixed season. It was made only for recognized brave men (A.L.K.). Sherer, "Great Chieftains," p. 26, calls this the Feather Ceremony, given presumably for the last time in 1947 upon the death of the last Great Chieftain, Sukulai homar (Pete Lambert). It was for "men who had lost their lives or devoted their lives for the benefit of the people, or whose ancestors for over one hundred years had earned this greatest of all Mojave tributes."

[18] It was where Aratêve lived: see n. 21, Episode 1.

[19] Quvkuvaka had farmland then, which had been covered with sand or gravel before 1903. The distance from Fort Mohave is five or six miles rather than nine, probably.

[1] Four were still alive; see above, Episode 6.

[2] The impulse is obsessive.

[3] These people, grieving, emotional, and expected to want revenge, are ready converts. "We shall be killed" of course means "we are ready to be killed if it goes that way."

[4] Significant, and probably true. The tribe knew the power of the soldiers' firearms. The threateners very likely consisted of the mourners plus the chronic belligerents.

[5] Kuyak-akwāΘ, a mile or two downstream from Fort Mohave, on the east side.

[6] The herdsman caring for sixteen mules belonging to Jacob Hall's company that had a contract to carry the mail from Kansas City, Missouri, to Stockton, California, via Beale's route: see Leroy Hafen, *The Overland Mail, 1849-1869* (Cleveland, 1926), pp. 115-116. This happened about July 20, about two-and-a-half miles south of the fort: Armistead's return, Fort Mohave, July 1859, in 617.

[7] Aha-kevāra, perhaps three miles below Fort Mohave.

By dark the horses were gone: everybody had one. And all the people whose houses were anywhere near the fort slipped out that night and went down river.

119. At that time there was no river at [what is now] Needles City: it flowed in a big bend far east in the valley. By daylight all the Mohave assembled at Kwa'orve,[8] then west of the river. They killed six horses there and ate them. Then they went on to Ah'a-kwinyevai,[9] then also "in California," [i.e., west of the river]. They stayed there six days. Then the war faction[10] said: "It is we that began to be bad.[11] Let us go fight them." On the sixth morning they started. They went up west of the river to Hatšioq-vātveve,[12] waiting for the rest [of the tribe]; then they all crossed to the east side at Hasoδape,[13] keeping close to the river bank in the brush; they were coming near Fort Mohave now.[14] At Hanyiko-tš-kwa'ampa,[15] they went behind the hill in the brush. It was nearly sundown.

120. Then the war leaders[16] said: "I want two or three men to go to the fort. When they see you, turn back and they will follow you."[17]

121. So five[18] men went, and when they came near the fort, they shouted and kicked up dust. The soldiers saw them and fell into formation: I could hear the sound of the drum. Now some of the Mohave were out in the open, on the [slope of the] mesa, [to the south]; others stayed in the brush below, [to the north]. I saw the soldiers come, though it was nearly dark: the lieutenant had a gray horse. The soldiers, on top of the mesa, did not see the Indians who were just below the brink, nor those below [and to the north behind] them. Now the first body of Mohave climbed up on the terrace from the south and the soldiers fired at them. Meanwhile the Mohave below to the north also came up and shot arrows; but the soldiers did not see them until one Mohave who had a gun fired and they heard it.[19] Then part of the soldiers faced about, so that they were firing in two directions. The Mohave attacking from the south were the first to turn: they all ran.[20] The soldiers' bullets struck the gravel which flew up and spattered them.

---

[8] Kwa'orve I cannot place. There is a Va'orve on the east edge of the valley more than half way from Needles to Topock, but that would be too far down.

[9] Ah'a-kwinyevai, almost north of Needles on the east side toward Spear Lake. The place is where Inyo-kutavêre narrated the *Mohave Historical Epic.*

[10] "The five" in my field notes.

[11] "Started trouble."

[12] Hatšioq-vātveve is about nine miles above Needles, on the same western side, where there was farmland.

[13] Hasoδape or Aha-soδape is opposite Hatšioq-vātveve, on the east side.

[14] Going upstream.

[15] Hanyiko-tš-kwa'ampa is up out of Mohave Valley on the mesa or up the slope of the Black Mountains somewhere east of the Needles-Fort Mohave line. The name means "Frog-emerge." Fleeing underground after bewitching the god Matavilya, Frog emerged three times, but still hearing wailing from Ha'avulypo, sank down again.

[16] "The five."

[17] Into an ambush.

[18] Five volunteers. This must have been the July 22 incident reported (in the July post return, in 617) by Armistead: "a party of Indians estimated from 150 to 200 appeared about 2½ miles below the Post. The Comdg. officer with twenty-three men went there fired on and dispersed them."

[19] The trap and skirmish in the dusk must have been picturesque.

[20] The "like-to-die" leaders seem to have run with them.

Then the northern body also broke and fled, back to the bushes in the low ground. No Mohave had been killed, nor any soldier either.[21]

122. That night they all crossed[22] [to the west side] to Hôkusave[23] and slept there.

123. In the morning they went[24] down river [and crossed] to Ahtôt-kwi-sakatve and Aha-qolinyo,[25] in Arizona southeast from where Needles City is now. One of the five warriors lived there;[26] it was to his place they all went. The mesquite beans were ripe [July-August] and that is what they lived on.

124. Ten days after the fight, four Mohave went back up along the [eastern] mountains[27] to scout. Now the soldiers had planted melons about a mile upriver from the fort; these were well along and growing. Coming down from the mountains, the Mohave cut off melons and pulled up vines most of the night. Then they returned and told what they had done.[28]

125. When the soldiers saw the damage they wanted to fight.[29] Eight of them started down river, late in the day. They stopped at Aha-kwa'ai.[30] Below there at Hwat-imāve, where Gus Spee[31] now lives [1903] is a good place to plant, and three Mohave were at work in their fields there [next morning]. Sneaking up just after sunrise, the eight soldiers saw them from close up and fired. They shot one of them through the thigh. His two companions dragged him to the river [which then ran] nearby, and jumped in.[32] The soldiers kept shooting but did not hit them again.

126. The [main body of] Mohave, down river, heard shouting: "The soldiers are coming," and started north. Then the eight soldiers retreated until they met their main body at Avi-uye-va.[33] The Mohave arrived there at midmorning and a battle

---

[21] Between ambuscade and dim light the soldiers evidently shot wildly; and, as for the Mohave, too many guns faced them to make a charge palatable.

[22] These crossings and recrossings go on interminably and are evidence of how aquatic the Mohave were, for the river is a great one.

[23] Hôkusave had houses, but they were abandoned, or uninhabited. It was where the god Mastamho turned into a bald eagle, according to one account (*Seven Mohave Myths,* p. 83). It is on the west side, about eleven miles above Needles, a little below where the Nevada line meets the river.

[24] They were getting farther away from the troops.

[25] Aha-qolinyo (or qwalinyo) is at the east foot of the valley, almost due east of Needles but several miles downstream from it, perhaps eight miles north of Topock.

[26] See Episodes 6 and 10 (A.L.K.). This would be a chief, To-pi-ko-na-ho (Brady's rendering), Tapaikunehe in Episode 1 here.

[27] The Black Mountains, a large, even range.

[28] Pure spite, and quite ineffective, but far from inconsequential, as the sequel shows.

[29] Soldiers did leave the fort by night, Aug. 4, but as the first move in a major strike—not in retaliation for loss of the melons.

[30] Aha-kwa'a'ï (see Episode 3). Hwat-imāve (see n. 31, Episode 9, below), and Avi-nye-va (n. 34, Episode 9, below) were close together on or near Spear Lake or Slough, northeast of Needles, near the east edge of the valley. The eight soldiers were those who first left the fort.

[31] As recorded. Evidently the settler for whom "Spear Lake" is named. We are now not far from Ah'a-kwinyevai (n. 9, Episode9, above), but farther east, away from the river.

[32] This begins the final clash between Mohaves and U.S. Army, reported by Armistead in his return for August 1859 (in 617). His larger force now left the fort, Aug. 5 in the morning, to surprise the Mohave. The first firing mentioned in the text is also reported by Armistead: [his group] "came on three Indians planting beans, about twelve miles below the Post—killed one. The firing raised the whole Valley."

[33] Avi-nye-va. It has the same name as Parker (see n. 59, below) (A.L.K.). The battle now

started. Some of the Mohave who so far had stayed quietly at home, now said: "Well, we will go in too,"[34] and they joined the fighting.

127. We[35] got to Ava-ke-hūmi, High-house.[36] Of the Mohave fighting, six had by then been killed and carried back down to this place, where all the Mohave were assembled. I saw the six dead men lying there naked, and three wounded. One man sat leaning against a post, with a shattered spine or pelvis. Another sat there, shot in the arm. And a third, hit in the leg, stood holding to a post. All were still; not a word was being said.[37]

128. Then a mere youth,[38] Tuvalykye-ahwata, one of the southern half of the Mohave, the Kavi-lya-δoma,[39] spoke [to the warriors]: "you own this [way of doing]. You like it to be like this, with dead men lying around. The whites treated you well, but you liked to die. Why don't you speak? The way you like to have it be, you have that now. Up here is the sun: I see it. But I will see it no more. When it goes down there, I will see it no longer. I will not see tomorrow. Why don't you take me with you? I want to die too."[40]

129. Thereupon a Matha-lya-δoma,[41] a Northern Mohave youth—Ara'ū-inyunye[42] was his name—also spoke. "Why don't you talk? Why don't you say something? When you fought, you would die, you said. 'In some wars they may chase me,' you said, 'but I know how to talk.' Well, why don't you talk before you die? I am a man and cannot live forever. A mountain lives on, and the river; the sun and the night keep coming on to us forever[43] every day. But any man whom you see dies; I will die too."[44]

130. Then the first of these two youths said: "I am ready," and the other said: "I am ready." Both had clubs. Then a great group followed them,[45] one company on the west, another on the east, and eight men farthest east.[46] When they came near

---

beginning would last about three hours and terminate with twenty-three known Mohave deaths, three of the army infantry being wounded: Armistead to General Clarke, Fort Mohave, August 6, 1859, in *Report, War, 1859,* pp. 419-420.

[34] Now that fellow tribesmen had been attacked.

[35] The reason for the change from "they" to "we" seems to signify that Chooksa homar is now reporting what he himself saw (C.B.K.).

[36] Named after a house there, taller than usual. I seem not to have recorded it as a settlement otherwise.

[37] One senses the tension in the silence. There was nothing the war inciters could say. Now two mere youths devote themselves—really—to death, and effect a rally.

[38] Mahai, a youth still unmarried, or, more likely, not yet a father; as masahai denotes a girl, married or unmarried, who is grown up but not yet a mother. Ordinarily, so young a man would not take charge or even speak up.

[39] "In-the-south-δoma." See n. 42, below; also the tribal names Hal-tsi-δoma, and [Maricopa] Kave-l-tsa-δom. While kave-k is "south" in Mohave, the underlying meaning seems to be "downstream," because the Maricopa applied Kave-l-tsa-δom to the tribe west of, below, them on the Gila.

[40] This is a sudden dedication under the stress of emotion, one feels, not a living up to an acquired repute or persona.

[41] "In-the-north-δoma." These two divisions of the Mohave seem to have been informal (see Episode 1 and explanation there of Professor Sherer's formulation of this).

[42] Ara'ū: his road?

[43] Night is frequently spoken of by the Mohave as "traveling" from the east like the sun.

[44] By charging the foe.

[45] They, not the chronic kwanami, are now the leaders.

[46] As given, but I do not know why this kind of formation.

the soldiers, the two youths charged, and the eight men charged, and [had] almost caught hold of the soldiers when these fired; and again they charged; and the soldiers almost fled. And the Mohave knelt and shot arrows.[47] Many of them were killed but the rest kept fighting. Then both youths were killed; and the rest fled. And at once the soldiers retreated, too.[48] And one of the [original] five who had got letters at Yuma was among the dead.[49]

131. I jumped into the tule rushes along with a companion. When the soldiers had left, I came out and saw the dead lying about. The wounded had been carried off, but the dead were left. I saw sixteen dead men lying where this fight had been.[50] No one was about; I and my companion were the first to get there. He went back and told the Mohave [they could] carry off their dead. Then ten men came and carried them away: some across the slough, some to Ava-ke-humī. They tore down the house there for firewood and cremated them.[51] The wounded were carried to their homes.[52]

132. "Some of you brave men said that if two or three got killed fighting, they would not mind; they liked that. Now many are dead. I don't want to stay in this place; I will go to Aha-kwaϴki.[53] If we stay here, the soldiers will come again and more will be killed. If the soldiers come to Aha-kwaϴki, we will go Ahany-uyā and cut tules for rafts and leave the country, so that they will not take our women and girls and children. Let the whites have this country."[54]

133. So they went to Aha-kwaϴki. The whole tribe was together in that one place for six days.

134. Aratêve talked to them. "You get angry sometimes; I know you are brave men and think you can beat anybody. You thought you could beat the whites: you said so. I told you you could not; the whites have beaten all tribes; all are friends to them now. You did not listen to what I said when I told you that. You did what you thought, and many have got killed. If the soldiers come, you cannot resist them. You did not know that, but now you know it. The country down river from here, which we took away from another tribe [the Halchidhoma], I will live there. Those of you who want to go on fighting can stay here. I do not want to and will leave you."[55]

135. Then they cut tule rafts and started. But Asikahôta [of the original war leaders] went to the foot of the valley, just above where Mellen is now, and said:

---

[47] And therewith lost the battle. Their one possible chance was to come to grips.

[48] It is not clear here whether the narrator saw the very last of the fighting. Armistead's account shows that he made two moves back toward the fort, with the Mohave interrupting the first of those moves with their final attack (C.B.K.).

[49] At last, after all the talk about it. But apparently only because the two youths led the attack at all (A.L.K.). This man was Ha-chur-ne-ah, as Brady says in his report of Oct. 9, 1860 (cit. supra). He was a chief living on the west side of the river, in the valley.

[50] Six before and sixteen now, plus wounded, is a genuine casualty list. Armistead counted twenty-three Mohave dead. Neither side stated how many wounded Mohaves later died.

[51] The soldiers might return, time was pressing, and the posts and rafters stood at hand.

[52] Presumably each to his own, so far as possible, but scarcely upstream?

[53] Aha-kwaϴki, "Pottery (vessel) water," is evidently well down in the valley, but I cannot place it.

[54] In his field notes A.L.K. did not attribute this speech, but he later assumed as do I that it was Yara tav speaking (as just below in the text).

[55] Aratêve definitely pulls out, even if the tribe splits.

"We[56] will stop here [for a while], we want to eat before we go on."[57] The others went on off down to Avi-nye-va,[58] the Parker region. The wounded lay on rafts with food beside them; unwounded people swam or waded alongside.

136. They got to the site of Parker in two days.[59] The Mohave already there,[60] hearing they were coming, built a big shade for them.[61] So they arrived: I was there.

EPISODE 10. PEACE AND RETURN

137. Then word came to them from those who were still in the Mohave Valley, from Asikahôta's people. A Yuma who spoke English, Ahan-kuta'êre,[1] said to him: "You are thinking the whites will attack you again, but I think not. It was that way at Yuma. The Yuma fought them and ran off, to Avatšohai,[2] and wanted to give up the war: the whites agreed, and the Yuma came home. That is how I think it will be with you: I know their way.[3] Go and see the commandant. Go upriver on the other side and hold up a handkerchief: that means you are not fighting any more. Put a letter[4] on a pole so they can see it. Then they will get you in a boat. They will not kill you; you will be friends again." Asikahôta asked: "They will not kill me?" "No, there will be no trouble," the Yuma told him.

138. Now [Asikahôta] stayed there, at Kuhuinye,[5] five days, then went upriver on the west side and did as he had been advised. The commandant, Yehumi-kw-ahwata, Beard-red,[6] saw him, and told two men to go over in a boat and take along Umpêre,[7] who spoke Mexican. "They won't fight any more," he said, "go on over!" So the three crossed and brought the five[8] Mohave to the fort to the commandant.

139. He asked: "Have you quit fighting?" Asikahôta[9] said: "Yes, we have quit. Some have gone to Parker."[10] 'Have they all gone there?" "No, only part." "Well, send someone, tell them all to come up, I want to talk with them. Tell them the war is over; they will understand and return. They are to come here."

---

[56] My party.

[57] Perhaps an excuse for delaying and separating.

[58] Not to be confused with the place of the same name, in n. 34, Episode 9, above.

[59] This is quick travel with women, children, aged, and wounded. Three days would be usual.

[60] Since the 1828 conquest, groups of Mohave had somewhat fitfully occupied and farmed parts of this, what was later called "Parker Valley." How many were there already in 1859 to receive these new arrivals, we do not know.

[61] For the wounded to convalesce under, in the torrid summer; or possibly to hold the commemoration for the slain.

[1] He is mentioned earlier, in Episode 7.

[2] Or Ava-tsūhai.

[3] As before, in Episodes 6 and 8.

[4] Letter, writing, paper: hanyora.

[5] Kuhuinye. I do not seem to have placed it (A.L.K.). Armistead says that the Mohaves "sent a runner into the Post and asked for peace," on August 24: August 1859 return, in 617.

[6] Armistead's nickname in Mohave?

[7] The white storekeeper, as in Episode 7.

[8] This tallies with Armistead's report: "From that time [August 24] until the 31st small parties of Indians have come into the Garrison." We notice that five occurs so often as to arouse a suspicion that it is a "round" number in secular situations as four is in ritual (C.B.K.).

[9] Here recorded as "Sukahot."

[10] As in Episode 9.

140. So Asikahôta sent word to them. But I was a youth then, not yet married.[11]

141. Those at Parker said: "Good. If they will not kill me it will be all right. The fighters are dead; those that did not want to live long have all been killed.[12] We will come, because we do not like fighting."

142. So they came upriver, with women and children, walking slowly; it took them three days to Mohave Valley.[13] Those who had fled there, came; those who had settled there before, stayed.

143. When they came back, the crops which they had planted at their homes were ripe.[14] After about two days, they all camped at Hakevare,[15] three miles below Fort Mohave. Next day they went to the fort to see the commandant.

144. "Are you all back?" he asked. "Yes, we are all here." "You will not fight any more?" "Yes."[16] "Don't do it!" "Yes. I was sorry to leave my land, that's why I came back. Now we are here, we will not fight any more." "If you do, we will take away your land and give it to white people. If any Indians are bad and kill someone, hand them over to me and I will put them into jail: that is how the whites do. On account of the two killed at Yuma, you all went to fight, and many were killed. Some of the Walapai are bad and fighting me. Don't help them! If they become worse, you and we will go to fight them." "Good. We are not bad any longer. When the Walapai are bad, tell us 'Kill them!' and we will do that." "Good. And you must stop killing stock. If you don't I shall have to jail you."

145. "I am going to appoint chiefs for you according to settlements,[17] to look after bad men who kill stock, and the mountain Indians that steal horses, Walapai and Chemehuevi. How many of you are ["captains"] chiefs?"

146. "This man." Then the commandant gave him a letter. He gave such letters to about ten men. Each one told where he lived and how many Indians lived with him: so they counted the Indians.[18] "That is why I was sent here: if you stop fighting, good, we stop; but if any are bad, we keep on until they are all killed."

147. Now these had their letters and everything was quiet; there was no trouble for eight years. The soldiers left,[19] to go to California. But some tribes still were bad,

---

[11] This was said in answer to a question from me. If Chooksa homar's own chronology of events is correct, he was about sixteen at the time.

[12] "All" is the customary exaggeration for "most" (A.L.K.). So far as we know, three of the original war-urgers were still alive (Homose-quahote, Koppetam, and To-pi-ko-na-ho: Brady mentions them all as of the fall of 1860).

[13] In Episode 9 they were seen to go down in two days, but then in flight. Three would be normal, with women and children, and under no pressure.

[14] August-September, since when they left the valley it was mesquite harvest season, July-August, as they reckoned things.

[15] Aha-kevare, "water without."

[16] On the logic of "Yes, we have no bananas" (A.L.K.). This final meeting took place August 31, 1859: Armistead to Gen. Clarke, Aug. 31, 1859, in *Report, War, 1859*, p. 421, and in his return for August in 617.

[17] Headmen of localities, perhaps of groups of kinsmen (A.L.K.). Armistead does not report having named chiefs or having issued letters. One wonders whether this was done later, by Major G. O. Haller, after he had Peter R. Brady's Oct. 9, 1860, report in hand.

[18] This census would be most illuminating if it happened to be preserved in the War Department archives in the National Archives (A.L.K.). My guess is that it is Peter Brady's report, Oct. 9, 1860, in 393 (C.B.K.).

[19] Evacuating Fort Mohave May 28, 1861, following Brig. Gen. E. V. Sumner's order of April 29, he perceiving that the post was useless, "no hostile Indians near it, and no traveling whatever on the

and there were complaints to the government, so the soldiers returned. Their commander was Colonel Price,[20] and he was at Fort Mohave three years. While the soldiers were away, the Walapai and Chemehuevi had killed white men.[21]

EPISODE 11. WAR WITH YAVAPAI AND WALAPAI

148. Then a white man named Lehigh (Līhai) came to Parker. Perhaps he was agent; anyway he wanted to do good to the Indians.[1] Now he went east to Ah'a-ikwisa'onve[2] to visit the Yavapai there.[3] He took along a young Mohave who spoke English; and he talked to the Yavapai.

149. When this was over, he returned and had come to Imitšaheba,[4] south of which is a mountain, and at the west end of this a spring; there he camped for the night. In the morning the Yavapai came: he heard them. The young Mohave knew it too; he ran and climbed the mountain. Then the Yavapai killed Lehigh.

150. They pursued the Mohave, calling: "We won't kill you. We only wanted to kill the white man, and he is dead. Come with us; we want you." So he came down to them; and they all gathered. Then they began to think: "If you let him go home, he will tell who killed the white man. Kill him too, then nobody will know. You have killed the [white] head man over the Indians and will have troops coming; you had better make away with him." The Mohave understood[5] them but could not escape. For three days they talked like this among themselves. Then they made a great fire, and when the sand was hot, they tied him hand and foot and laid him on the sand to cook. In the morning he was done and they ate

---

road it was intended to protect": quoted in William A. Keleher, *Turmoil in New Mexico, 1846-1868* (Santa Fe, 1952), p. 216.

[20] Lt.-Col. William Redwood Price arrived at and took command of the fort on June 14, 1867: his letter of June 16 in *Walapai Papers* (Washington, D.C., 1936), p. 41.

[21] As will appear in later episodes of this reminiscence.

[1] George W. Leihy was appointed Superintendent of Indian Affairs March 3, 1865, the day the Colorado River Reservation was created on paper. By that time Yara tav and many Mohave were living on those lands.

[2] Ah'a-ikwisa'onve (ah'a is cottonwoods) is "4 days on horseback from Mohave Valley, E of Big Sandy, W of Prescott." It is almost certainly the same as Ahakisa-unva which Gifford, *Northeastern and Western Yavapai*, UCPAAE 34 (Berkeley, 1936), 255, cites as a spot to which the Northeast Yavapai of Cordes, Cleator, and Mayer came to gather giant cactus fruit and palo verde seeds earlier than elsewhere. The three localities from which they came are twenty to thirty miles southeast of Prescott. Gifford informed me that Blind Indian Creek is perhaps fifteen miles over a divide to the southwest, almost due south of Prescott, and that it is an affluent of upper Hassayampa "river," a little below Walnut Grove. Ahakisa-unva thus is almost on the boundary (Gifford, map) between Northeast and Western Yavapai claims. It would thus be just about four days riding from Mohave Valley, but would be far southeast of the Big Sandy instead of between it and Prescott.

[3] These would be Northeastern Yavapai, not of the Western, Tolkepaya division on Williams and Santa Maria rivers and south thereof (A.L.K.). John Feudge, agent to the Colorado River Indians, reporting from La Paz, Dec. 15, 1866, said that Leihy had with him his clerk; a friendly Maricopa interpreter; and an Apache Mojave (i.e., Yavapai, perhaps a Northeastern Yavapai) whom Leihy was returning to his own band for punishment there: *Report, Indian Affairs, 1867*, p. 167.

[4] Imitšaheba seems unplaced on any map (A.L.K.). Feudge stated that this happened about twelve miles from Prescott, at Bell's ranch, on November 18, 1866.

[5] The languages are partially intelligible.

him—not the whole of him, but a little. Some men[6] did that when they took prisoners: it is called YakaΘa'alye.[7]

151. Now no one knew of this: the Mohave at Parker thought Lehigh would come back. Then it was two years. Lehigh had money with him: greenbacks, checks, silver, gold, to pay the Mohave for making ditches at Parker. A Chemehuevi married to a Yavapai woman had got one of the checks and kept it for two years.[8] Then he took it to Ehrenberg[9] and tried to cash it. "Where did you get it?" He would not tell. "He is the one that killed Lehigh," and they put him in jail, I don't know where. And soldiers came to La Paz.[10] Now Aratêve said: "All right, I will see about it; I'll arrange something."[11]

152. So he went to the Yavapai country, to Ah'a-ikwisa'onve. He said to them: "I will tell you something that is going to be. There will be what you have never seen. There will be irrigation ditches and schools and other things. The government told me that. Will you go see the government?" The Yavapai chief, Môδata-'ôletši,[12] agreed. "You will come for sure?" "Yes." "You will come in six days? Surely? I will tell them so." "Yes, we will surely come."

153. Then Aratêve returned[13] and told the authorities. And in six days the Yavapai arrived, thirty or forty of them, without women, all men; and the government [officers] gave them rations, which they cooked and ate. The

---

[6] I started to write "some Mohave" in my notes, presumably because my interpreter habitually said "Indians" when he meant Mohave; then changed to "some Indians," which would mean "tribes other than Mohave." I have no other reference to the custom as being Mohave. The Yavapai have previously been charged with ritual cannibalism: Spier, *Yuman Tribes*, p. 178; Gifford, *"Northeastern and Western Yavapai,"* p. 304; and his *The Southeastern Yavapai*, UCPAAE 29 (Berkeley, 1932), 186.

[7] YakaΘa'alya is what the Mohave would call their own victory dance over a scalp: Kroeber, *Handbook*, p. 752. The torture killing is evidently regarded as the Yavapai equivalent. Royal Stratton's account of the Oatman captivity pictures the Mohave torturing and killing an escaped but recaptured Cocopa woman slave or prisoner. This has been discussed in A. L. Kroeber, "Olive Oatman's Return."

[8] Presumably unaware of the difference between paper money and checks?

[9] Agent Tonner to Supt. Herman Bendell, Colorado River Reservation, Dec. 20, 1871, and Bendell's note from Prescott, Jan. 20, 1872, Records of the Arizona Superintendency of Indian Affairs, 1863-1873, USNA (hereinafter cited as 734), reporting Mohave changing fifty-dollar and one hundred-dollar bills at the La Paz post office (Mohave acting for Yavapai). General Crook soon knew of it: *General George Crook, His Autobiography* (Norman, Okla. 1946), p. 174; and Indian Agent J. Williams to Supt. Bendell, Camp Date Creek, Oct. 1, 1872, in 734. James Barney, *Tales of Apache Warfare* (Phoenix, 1933), pp. 19-20, who was present for some of the pertinent events in 1872, says that some of the Yavapai who killed George Leihy in Nov. 1866 were the same people who ambushed a stage near Wickenburg, Nov. 5, 1871, and took the greenbacks referred to above. Barney could be right, at least in that the coincidence was believed at the time, since Agent Williams mentions it in his letter cited above. But insofar as this Mohave reminiscence is concerned, it looks as if Chooksa homar telescoped the two ambushes in his own mind (C.B.K.).

[10] La Paz was on the east side of the river, six or seven miles above Ehrenberg, which was due east and directly across the River from Blythe. Troops came to La Paz too often to give us a firm date from these words alone. My guess is that Chooksa homar is again talking about late 1866 or 1867. A detachment of troops was brought in to La Paz very soon after the Quashackama ambush and stayed there almost continuously through 1872 and even later.

[11] The motivation may have been political ambition, pressure from whites with whom he wished to stand well, or revenge for the Mohave who had disappeared.

[12] "Shame-cooked"—a name of the frivolously obscene type.

[13] To La Paz? Or to Parker?

Yavapai chief [kept] saying: "I know it but can do nothing: [I feel] as if they were standing all around me."[14] In the morning the soldiers had them surrounded and shot and killed them all, the chief too; not one escaped.[15]

154. Then the Yavapai in the mountains fought, and the Walapai too, and killed whites, broke up wagons, took livestock; and the soldiers went out against them.

155. Then [some][16] Mohave told the troops: "I know the springs at which they live." So they went with the soldiers and helped them hunt the Yavapai and Walapai. They did that for four or five months. Some of the Yavapai[17] escaped and went to the Yuma, who hid them.

156. Asakyêt,[18] a Mohave brave man and chief who was with the Americans in this fighting, went to the Yuma chief who had the Yavapai [refugees concealed], and this chief told him where they were—for no one would protect them if he knew they were bad.[19] So Asakyêt went there, killed two or three, and captured their chief, successor of the one killed;[20] he was Tšimevêve-isalye, "Chemehuevi-hand."[21] He took him on the steamboat to Parker, and there the agent kept him—Kanafyutš was the agent's name, but the Mohave called him Kanahyutš.[22]

157. A year after this Yavapai chief had been captured, the Walapai were still fighting on. Asakyêt was thinking about it, and said to the authorities: "I will see

[14] Presentiment. He must have realized that he was trapped if the whites acted in bad faith. They had perhaps not heard of Leihy's death, for all he knew; but they might have.

[15] This may be the unprovoked murder of somewhere between eight and fifteen Yavapai, done either Sept. 24 or 25 on the outskirst of La Paz. The significance of the event was the death of the Western Yavapai chief, Quashackama upon whom Indian agents and Yara tav's Mohave depended heavily for mediation with various Yavapai groups that came to and went from the River Reservation. See *Arizona Miner,* Oct. 3, 1868; Ralph H. Ogle, *Federal Control of the Western Apaches, 1848-1886* (Albuquerque, 1940), pp. 71-72 and sources he cites; and Superintendent G. W. Dent to General E. O. C. Ord, San Bernardino, Calif., Sept. 22, 1868, in 734.

[16] A.L.K. wondered whether the reference here was to Yara tav, or Asukit, that is, whether to Mohaves living on the River Reservation or near Fort Mohave.

[17] This suggests personal friendships, and possibly also that the refugees were southerly Tolkepaya (Western Yavapai).

[18] Asukit (picked cactus fruit) of the Neolge clan was, according to Lorraine Sherer, "Great Chieftains," p. 32, War Chief of the Mojaves in 1859, which she states to have been a hereditary position. He was a kwanami and began to be figured as a chief by the whites at some time during the 1860s or early 1870s, from which I assume that he was elected to one of the hereditary chieftainships in Mojave Valley. He scouted for General Crook and Prof. Sherer states that he was Indian Peace Officer of the Fort Mojaves after the wars ended. He was later one of two temporary principal chiefs (in effect, regents during a king's minority), 1888-1896, and he died in 1899.

[19] This naiveté may have been put in for me and a potential audience of whites. Or it may be palliation of the breach of sanctuary.

[20] We have found no mention of this episode in white's records. Presumably the reference here is to Môðata-'ôletši.

[21] The usual order in noun compounds is the reverse of this (A.L.K.). The man was well remembered by Yavapai to whom Edward Gifford talked in the early 1930s. He was one of the (nonhereditary) chiefs, and the earliest anyone could then recall by name.

[22] There is bilabial *v*, but no *f* in Mohave: I cannot reconstruct the English form of this name (A.L.K.). There was no agent of such name. The man may be John Feudge, known familiarly as "Colonel." If only people had called him "kunlfee-udge," then this Kanafyuts would sound very much like. But the only test of this possibility I know is in a letter by the government farmer on the River Reservation, who referred to the agent as "Curnel Fuge": A. J. Myers to Dent, Alamo Bonito on the Reservation, July 30, 1867, in 734. The only time I know when this chief took his people down to

if I can bring them in." "Good, try what you can do." So he went to the Walapai country, though the war was still on, and said: "Some soldiers are coming to talk, not to kill. I am here because I want you to come and stay in our country. We have not seen you for a long time and want you to quit fighting."[23] "All right, we will quit," they said. "Good, I will tell the government," he said and returned to the river.

158. Then the Walapai came to the Mohave houses across from [where] Needles [is now]. Some wanted to put them all in one house and kill them in that. But Asakyêt said: "If you do that, some will escape because they will know what you mean to do. Let them move about [and scatter] where they like, visit their friends."[24] Then it was done that way: they lived and ate with the Mohave; the crops were nearly ripe.

159. Then they were ready to kill the Walapai. There were twenty Mohave and twenty soldiers: I was with them.[25] Then they went to every settlement at which Walapai were sleeping, killed the men and captured the women.[26] Opposite Needles was a large settlement with many Walapai in it. The headman who [had] kept[27] them said: "I will tell the Mohave women in the same house with Walapai[28] to leave; if they are mixed up, you cannot tell them apart." So he went back and had the Mohave leave.[29]

160. Asakyêt said: "Let these Mohave go indoors and fight them. Don't shoot, soldiers, else you will be hitting Mohave. If some one runs and we call out that he is a Walapai—only then shoot." When they were near the house, the twenty Mohave ran hard and leaped indoors. The Walapai knew what was coming and were awake. They had clubs and fought without trying to run: they seized each others' hair and struck: it was too close to shoot: they fought a long time like that.[30] The Mohave [came out and] said: "We can't kill them all: it is too dark

---

the river to avoid troops and settlers was late in 1872 or early in 1873: see John G. Bourke, *On the Border with Crook* (Columbus, Ohio, 1950: orig. publ. 1891), p. 171, and Superintendent Bendell to Agent Tonner, Prescott, March 7, 1873, in 734; perhaps also a distorted reference to the same movement, in *Weekly Arizona Miner,* March 29, 1873.

[23] The episode that follows must represent the ambush carried out on one of the last days of September or very early in October 1866 in retaliation for killings of miners by Walapais who had recently moved into Mohave Valley. See *Weekly Arizona Miner,* Oct. 13 and Nov. 10, 1866; Agent Feudge's long letter from La Paz, Oct. 16, 1866, in 734; and his brief letter from La Paz, June 30, 1867, in *Report, Indian Affairs, 1867,* pp. 160-161. That the Walapais had been ready, even earlier, to kill nearby whites, is reported by the acting commander of Fort Mohave, Lt. Dan Loosley, April 19, 1866, in 734. Lorraine Sherer discusses this incident cogently in "Great Chieftains," p. 10, pointing to its significance as indicating whites' attempting to use Mojave against Walapai, with consequent accusations that the Mohave were now "collaborators." See Discussions, for more detailed consideration.

[24] Lulling suspicion.

[25] Meaning that he took part? It hardly accords with the rest of his behavior. Perhaps he only meant that he was there and saw what happened.

[26] One wonders whether the U.S. Army really had a hand.

[27] Treachery, even of a host.

[28] Walapai women, or Walapai husbands or lovers?

[29] Which could hardly have been done without warning the Walapai inside, as we see in the next paragraph.

[30] The houses were pitch dark; if there had been a small fire, it was banked with sand.

inside." Six Walapai were killed and two Mohave;[31] and the Mohave had taken Walapai captives, women and boys. The rest of the Walapai men escaped.[32]

161. Among the dead Walapai was Apānas, a "bad" man and brave, who exhorted them to stand. He was no chief, but he knew that if they fled the soldiers would shoot them.[33] One Walapai had a bow; it was he who killed the two Mohave.

162. A year after this, the Yavapai returned to their homes around Aha'-ikwisa'onve.[34] They thought all fighting had stopped. The whites saw them there. The captured Yavapai chief[35] had been killed at La Paz by the soldiers.[36] But it was the wrong man they killed. The actual murderer[37] of Lehigh had not been caught.

163. Aratêve said: "I will do it [for you]. I will go to the Yavapai, call them, and give them tobacco. I will hand it to the murderer, so you will know him. And I will hand it to all their bad men. Then I will wave a handkerchief and you can seize them."[38] So he did that, and Asakyêt was with him. So the soldiers got all their bad men.[39]

164. Some of the Yavapai said: "I will not let them take my relatives." They seized their bows and fought. Then the soldiers shot most of them. The Yavapai were once a big tribe,[40] but after they had been slaughtered twice, most of them were gone.

165. The survivors were taken to San Carlos[41] and kept on the reservation there. The Mohave took some Yavapai women as slaves—some to Needles, some to Parker.[42] The Yavapai were kept at San Carlos a long time, until they said they

---

[31] Casualties reported to Agent Feudge were twenty-one Walapais (the newspaper reported twenty-six), and one Mohave.

[32] Not clear how. They may have tunneled out from the back of the house and dashed into brush. Or were the soldiers ashamed to keep up a guard until daylight?

[33] He was right.

[34] See mention of the same location above, Episode 11, n. 2: Blind Indian Creek, per Gifford, and in Albert H. Schroeder, *A Study of Yavapai History*, 2 (3 parts, Santa Fe, 1959), p. 65.

[35] This appears to be "Chemehuevi-hand" as above; but there may have been a confusion in the original transcription of this remark, since this chieftain lived on at least until 1873 or 1874. I am guessing that Chooksa homar in 1903 meant to refer back to the Quashackama killing at La Paz (C.B.K.).

[36] So also here: the same chief would not have been kept by the agent, and killed by soldiers. The narrator must be referring to the Quashackama ambush in September 1868 for the moment (C.B.K.).

[37] Or murderers.

[38] This very brief report accurately conveys Yara tav's role at the Camp Date Creek meeting of Sept. 8, 1872, in which General George Crook was trying among other things to entrap the Yavapai who had ambushed the stage carrying the "Loring Party" near Wickenburg, Nov. 5, 1871. See *Weekly Arizona Miner,* Sept. 14, 1872; U.S. Indian Agent J. Williams to Supt. Bendell, Camp Date Creek, Oct. 1, 1872, and Bendell's letter of Sept. 30, 1872, both in 734.

[39] Not necessarily. A free-for-all resulted when Yara tav had "tagged" the guilty Yavapai by handing them tobacco, and very shortly thereafter all the Indians not dead or incarcerated had left the camp (C.B.K.).

[40] The ensuing hostilities are summarized briefly in Bourke, and detailed by Ogle, pp. 109-117.

[41] First from Camp Date Creek to the Verde Reservation (May 1, 1873, and later for groups trapped during the next two months); then, beginning Feb. 27, 1875, they were transferred to the San Carlos Reservation: Ogle, pp. 120, 126.

[42] Did the military wink at this, or not know about it? At any rate, the taking of women captives evidently held a great attraction for these tribes.

would be peaceable. Then the Americans let them out and gave them a little land at Ahtše-kwiδuke, between Yuma and Phoenix;[43] they are there now [in 1903].

EPISODE 12. WAR WITH THE CHEMEHUEVI

166. Now everything was right for two years. Then the Chemehuevi turned bad.[1] It was because they thought they could whip [us] that they made trouble. Two of them came to the foot of the valley, near Mellen [Topock] and killed a woman who was working[2] akatai seeds. They killed her without reason.[3] Then her husband, Kwarve'itšiδoma, said: "The government says it is not good to fight, but to be friends. So I have been going around and talking with all tribes. But now these Chemehuevi came and killed my wife. I think that is bad. I want to fight the Chemehuevi if you think it is right. But I will not fight them unless you say so." Then the government—that was Colonel Price[4] at Fort Mohave—said: "That was a bad thing to do. But I can't catch them in the mountains. So you go and fight them." Then a Chemehuevi came alone and the Mohave killed him.

167. Now Aratêve called for a hundred young men[5] to go up to Cottonwood Island where Chemehuevi were living. He got three white men to go along, also three white soldiers, one of whom cooked.[6] They went up to Hardyville, six miles upriver from Fort Mohave, where there was a ferry,[7] and crossed to the Nevada side, and kept going upstream. The Chemehuevi had left and were in the mountains. One of them was caught and killed by the Mohave. Whenever they

---

[43] Chooksa homar thought this might be the Gila Bend Reservation, as he put it.

[1] In 1864 like other Paiute they were harrassing white travelers on the Fort Mohave-Los Angeles route, and ambushing individual miners along and near the Colorado River: see Capt. Chas. Atchisson, commanding Fort Mohave, letters of June 22 and Aug. 23, 1864, in 234, and Feb. 20 and March 5, 1865, Fort Mohave, Letters Sent, 1863-1866, in 393. In Feb.- March, 1865, the army tried to nip all this in the bud by taking Chemehuevi hostages, but found no Indians in Chemehuevi Valley: *Alta California,* April 3, 1865 [Arizona Pioneers' Historical Society transcript: hereinafter APHS] for a letter of March 20, 1865, from a California Volunteer soldier on this expedition. The army established several temporary posts, notably Camp Cady, and some north of Fort Mojave toward Utah, and engaged in several years of hostilities west and north of Mojave country that could be called the Paiute War. For research on Camp Cady and associated problems, see Leonard Waitman, "The History of Camp Cady," *Quarterly Publication of the Historical Society of Southern California,* 36 (March, 1954), 49-91.

[2] In March 1865: see discussion in Arthur Woodward, "Iritaba—'Chief of the Mohave'," *Plateau,* 25 (Jan. 1953), 64.

[3] The Mohave opinion or version.

[4] Lt.-Col. Wm. R. Price went to Fort Mohave in June 1867.

[5] And presumably got them. This was likely to be exciting, and there was provocation. This occurred in September 1865: see Woodward, "Iritaba," pp. 64-66, and sources he cites; and Supt. George Leihy in *Report, Indian Affairs, 1865,* p. 503. Woodward's account parallels Chooksa homar's closely.

[6] A.L.K. said "This 'soldier' cooking on an Indian war party is something to wonder about." My guess is that the one cooking for two others seemed notable to Chooksa homar because Mohave on war expeditions tended to travel with just a little dry food to tide them over.

[7] An enterprise of William Harrison Hardy, who briefly recounts his 1865 ferry and toll-road activities there, in Tucson *Arizona Daily Citizen,* March 29, 1867 [APHS]. See his contract with Walapai chiefs Wauba Yuma, Hitchie-Hitchie, and Sherum [Tokoomhet] for the Mohave and Prescott Toll Road Company, to use Walapai country through from Hardyville on the river to Juniper Pass environs: July 15, 1865, in *Walapai Papers,* p. 34.

came near the Chemehuevi, these fled. So they kept chasing them and went a long way. Aratêve and a white man were mounted, [got ahead of the rest, and suddenly found they had] come among the Chemehuevi. Aratêve said: "I am not trying to kill you but to be friends, only you would not wait."[8] Some of them wanted to shoot him, others said "Don't." So they all stood around. Aratêve was wearing a tasseled suit and a big hat he had got in Washington.[9] He gave these[10] to the Chemehuevi chief: "My friend, we do not fight." When he started to return, the Chemehuevi shot at him but missed. It was a rocky place where the horses could not run well. Then the white man with him jumped off and ran on foot and nearly was caught. So the two returned, when it was nearly sundown, to Selye'ai-ihtata[11] on Cottonwood Island. At that time Chemehuevi and Mohave both lived there, but fewer Mohave;[12] and these returned to the valley the next day with Aratêve's party.

168. The same day the Mohave at the lower end of the valley attacked some Chemehuevi living at MataΘo[13] in Chemehuevi Valley.[14] There were no whites with these Mohave, but five Yavapai.[15] The Chemehuevi heard them coming and fled up into the mountains. The Mohave followed, and they fought with arrows.[16] Of the Chemehuevi none was killed, but they killed a Mohave. The two parties returned to the valley on the same day. With one Chemehuevi killed in the north and one Mohave in the south, things were even.

---

[8] The same old story, told as soon as the foes are the more numerous.

[9] He left for Washington probably in November 1863 and returned in May 1864, sponsored by John Moss, and probably accompanied all the way by Antonio Azul of the Pima. Attempts to locate reports of his visits in New York City and Washington, D.C., and putative talk with Abraham Lincoln, have not borne fruit. Arthur Woodward, in *Feud on the Colorado,* reproduces the only known photograph, Yara tav still wearing the huge cocked hat and other paraphernalia, posing with Ah-hotch-o-cama, the West Yavapai chief-of-band who often came to the Colorado River. See plate 10.

[10] The whites' account say he had to lay aside all this clothing, and as A.L.K. remarked, this "must have been undignified, in front of a hostile audience."

[11] "Ihtata-sand." Cottonwood Island, or more properly Islands, began about twenty and ended about twenty-five miles above Fort Mohave, with a maximum width of a mile or more. As Aratêve came back to it, he must have ridden even farther (A.L.K.). Woodward, *Feud on the Colorado,* says all this happened about twenty miles north of the island.

[12] Thus other accounts also. It probably afforded a better living agriculturally than most Chemehuevi territory, but not as good as the big Mohave or Parker valleys.

[13] MataΘo is Amat-AΘove, a Chemehuevi settlement with some farm patches, near the Colorado River in Chemehuevi Valley (A.L.K.). From here on there are few concordances between whites' and narrator's accounts. I indicate some of the difficulties in Discussions, below; and in making the footnotes that follow I have been assuming that Chooksa homar was much better informed of events in Mohave Valley than he was of what was passing on the River Reservation.

[14] This is a much smaller valley than Mohave Valley, especially in the amount of naturally-flooded farm land. The Chemehuevi crept into it from the west, some time after the eighteenth century, especially after the expulsion of the Halchidhoma from the Colorado to the Gila (about 1828) left a populational void between the Mohave and Yuma tribes. James O. Pattie in passing by there in 1826 or 1827 does not mention anyone there.

[15] Presumably some West Yavapai, some of whom spent part of each year on the Colorado River, to farm, to collect food there, to visit, and, more and more as time went on, to avoid trouble nearer their homes.

[16] A.L.K. wrote: "It seems strange that neither side had guns at that late date." Woodward, "Iritaba," notes that Mohaves borrowed some firearms from whites, for the September 1865 attack. The Paiute by that time often had at least a few guns.

169. Now the Mohave were afraid[17] of the Chemehuevi and all gathered to live together near Fort Mohave.[18] And the Chemehuevi, when they moved from mountain to mountain, went far to the north or south: none of them were about close by any more.

170. Two years later, some Chemehuevi came from the south to the Mohave and said: "I want no more fighting; I want to be friends, and to see the government." They came to the fort and told the same thing, that they would not fight the Mohave any longer. The government[19] approved.

171. That Chemehuevi chief's name was Θenyô-hiv'auve.[20] When he returned to his home in the mountains to the south, he told his people there: " 'I will not fight any longer, I am friends,' so I said to the Mohave, and they answered 'Good!' But they do not know what I think. I think[21] I want to kill them. I wanted to see their houses and where they live. Well, I saw them all."[22] Then he notified all the Chemehuevi to assemble at his place in two months.[23]

172. So they came across the country and gathered, and at Chemehuevi Valley they crossed to Arizona and went [north] around the Needles Peaks, and [on up] into the mountains on a mesa about four miles east of Mellen [Topock],[24] where they camped.

173. Next midmorning the Mohave, playing hoop-and-poles in the open,[25] saw them coming. Some ran [to the houses] to get their bows and arrows; others, who had none, broke their gaming poles to club with.[26] The Chemehuevi stood

---

[17] Even though the numbers were in their favor. Apparently they were without reprisals against the Chemehuevi ability to strike out of the unknown and then disappear into the desert or mountains. C.B.K. has seen no awareness of this fear in records by the whites near Fort Mohave; for evidence of it on the reservation, see Supt. Leihy's letter of Feb. 1, 1866, in 734.

[18] Probably in the shelter of the fort, or within range of its protection. There was good farmland close by.

[19] The Indian agents often tried to mediate in such situations. But one problem here (see Discussions, below) is whether the narrator was referring to the unauthorized treaty of March 21, 1867, signed at the reservation by Yara tav and Pan Coyer (As-pan-ku-yah): see copies with Annual Report, Department of the Pacific, AGO, and with Supt. Dent's letter of April 1, 1867, in 234—and now published in Robert F. Heizer and Alan Almquist, *The Other Californians* (Berkeley, Calif., 1971).

[20] The name is Mohave: either a translation or an epithet or nickname applied by them.

[21] *"Think,"* meaning *"intend," "mean," "wish."*

[22] "All," signifying "many "

[23] Why so long? One would have thought that in two months the secret would have been spilled. But in their fictitious clan history the Mohave set similar terms for their war rendezvous: see Kroeber, *A Mohave Historical Epic,* pp. 155, 157. And this Chemehuevi chief may have wanted to lull suspicion by an interval of peace and induce the Mohave to scatter away from the protection of Fort Mohave—as they did.

[24] Four miles east would be south of the Sacramento Wash which the railroad follows, but they may have crossed the wash and camped northeast of Topock so as to be nearer the Mohave settlements, which stretched upriver from Topock (A.L.K.). I am assuming that the attack about to be detailed in the text was the one reported to Agent John Feudge, as having occurred about June 18, 1866, in south Mohave Valley: Feudge to Leihy, La Paz, July 5, 1866, in 734.

[25] Unfortunately I did not record the name of the settlement. It might have been Atsquqa, Sampuly-kuvāra, KwiΘa'ôka, or Avi-tšîtse on the east side. They were back home from Fort Mohave on the strength of the Chemehuevi profession of friendship.

[26] The Yuma are described by Spier via the Maricopa as fighting with long clubs, against mass attacks (*Yuman Tribes,* pp. 171, 173). There were also the intratribal stick fights of Mohave contesting in disputes over land: see Kroeber, *Handbook,* p. 745. The gaming poles were too long to beat with, and stabbing habits seem to have been foreign to those river tribes.

near them [and shot]. There were too many of them: the Mohave were few, only from five or six houses.[27] So they fought there. Two Mohave women were killed, a girl, and two men; and two boys were scalped without being killed: they took only part of their hair,[28] and one of these boys is still living [in 1903].

174. Now word was being sent upriver to Fort Mohave, but it was far, twenty miles,[29] and it took nearly all day for help to arrive.[30] The twenty-five or so Mohave did not run off, but fought all day,[31] as the sun got lower.

175. About four o'clock a Mohave woman ran and swam the river to the California side. Now additional Chemehuevi, about fifty of them, had come to that side expecting to find Mohave living there.[32] But finding nobody, they just stayed around.[33] Now when this woman arrived, they shot her and threw her [back] into the river. She let herself float down, then drew out four or five arrows,[34] [and escaped:] she is still living.

176. Then all the Chemehuevi [who had been fighting] crossed over to the California side with horses they had captured and went on up into the mountains.[35] Now a large body of Mohave arrived where the fighting had been, and they too crossed the river, in pursuit, but could not catch up with the Chemehuevi, who had got too far up into the mountains. So the Mohave all returned to where the five people had been killed and helped burn them.[36] And the Chemehuevi went to their homes [at a distance.]

177. A year later [some of] the Chemehuevi returned to Chemehuevi Valley [to live], but without having made peace. The soldiers were still at Fort Mohave at this time.

178. Now two Mohave went to Chemehuevi Valley and saw fires burning. But they saw no people, and nobody came near them. [This was because] the Chemehuevi were indeed farming in the valley on its western side, but at night always went back into the mountains. So Mohave coming upriver from Parker never saw them, though they did see fires at night. These two Mohave however

---

[27] At four or five to a house this might mean twenty to thirty men of fighting age, with which the next paragraph agrees: its "twenty-five or so" is evidently an estimate, not a count.

[28] Pieces of scalp were evidently cut or torn hastily while fighting was still going on.

[29] The airline distance from Topock to Fort Mohave is about twenty-five miles. Perhaps the majority of the tribe were still in the north.

[30] Whoever carried the message probably got a horse before he had gone far; and presumably part of the advance guard of relieving Mohave were mounted, though not necessarily—they were a foot-traveling, foot-fighting people and proud of it.

[31] This tough defensive fighting with always a hope of coming to close quarters was their tradition. Meanwhile no doubt they sheltered themselves or dodged, arrows, shot arrows back, and were hit by a good many. Their own were merely arrowweed (*Pluchea*) rods, without stone, bone or hardwood tips: these were easily manufactured by dozens or hundreds. The Chemehuevi chipped stone heads for shooting deer and mountain sheep, but their fighting arrows may have been like those of the Mohave: Kroeber, *Handbook*, p. 597.

[32] West-side settlements were relatively few in the valley below Needles. The annually flooded farmlands mostly lay east of the river. There is similar though less disproportion above Needles.

[33] Such planlessness in the face of contingencies is probably typical of most groups not led by authority.

[34] This suggests they were of untipped arrowweed.

[35] Where they felt at home, as against the Mohave.

[36] Cremation always took place as soon after death as possible (A.L.K.). I am assuming that many Chemehuevi were living in Southern California during late 1866 and early 1867, accounting for the narrator's two remarks just below in the text. They may have been with the Cahuilla at that time.

arrived during the day [and went on] and came on a Chemehuevi house and stayed a while talking, saying they would all be friends and relatives. They said that to deceive them because they were afraid of being killed.[37]

179. When they returned, they told the Mohave: "Yes, the Chemehuevi have come back to the valley to live." So it was decided to attack them and word was sent to all in the tribe.

180. They gathered near Mellen, started down river in the morning, and in the afternoon crossed to the California side at Hamatyême,[38] near where the Chemehuevi were. There they waited ["camped"] until midnight, then walked on slowly, so as to reach the Chemehuevi houses at daylight. Some of the Chemehuevi still slept up in the mountains, but some were staying here: three young men, an old man, an old woman, a young woman with a little girl, seven in all. The Mohave killed the four men and seized the old woman and the child, but the younger woman was angry, refused to come along, bit and kicked when they took her by the hand, threw sand and sticks.[39] "We can't take her," they all said and shot her. So that made two of the seven whom they took prisoners, and with them they returned. "The other Chemehuevi are way up in the mountains," they reported, "and we don't know in which."

181. The Chemehuevi out from there did not go back into Chemehuevi Valley, but to Parker, where they lived at Avi-nye-kutapaive.[40] Their chief was called Apaily-kmaⴁ'e,[41] who wore chickenhawk feathers as insignia of bravery, as among the Mohave: he wore them in a big bunch on his head and then falling down to the knee.[42] The young Chemehuevi wanted to go on with the war,[43] and he said: "You young men want to fight—well, I can't stop you."

182. Among the Mohave living near there [but] in Arizona who heard of this was a brave man Itšiyêre-ⴁūme.[44] He said: "The Chemehuevi think they only are men. Others are men too. I am a man. I do not like to fight, but, well, I will fight also. It is bad men who fight, but I am not bad."

183. So, [under his leadership] they went to where the Chemehuevi lived, who saw them coming and got out their feathers[45] and bows. The Mohave called out:

---

[37] Like Aratêve, in section 167 above. The wonder is that such statements were ever believed.

[38] Unidentified. Misheard for Amat-yême?

[39] Anger overriding prudence: perhaps her husband or brother had just been killed. We have no report from whites' sources.

[40] Avi-nye-kutapaive, "below Parker," home for a year in the early nineteenth century of the Kohuana tribe: Kroeber, *Handbook*, p. 800 (A.L.K.). There is a sort of hiatus in the whites' records that extends through the last part of 1868 and until the first sure indication of Chemehuevi having reoccupied the west-bank lands opposite Parker, in July 1869.

[41] Or Apaly-kwaⴁ'ê. This name also seems to be Mohave.

[42] Like a Plains "war bonnet," but perhaps in two pieces, a spherical head dress plus a feathered strip. In the symbolism of the region, hawks counted for more than eagles: warriors dreamed of them.

[43] The young got the blame, anyway. However much he himself wanted to fight, he could not have done much without support of the youthful ones.

[44] Bird(s)—ⴁume.

[45] One begins to think that the naive white American's notion that the Indians can fight only when painted and feathered might after all be near the mark (A.L.K.). This attack does not appear in whites' records we have seen, but it fits with the tenor of Dodt's reports from summer through winter 1869. The Chemehuevi were now doing a lot of damage to the agency, seeming to the Mohave to press in and to threaten a coming disaster. As-pan-ku-yah asked, probably late in October 1869 to bring his people on the reservation lands, his people being in starving condition: Supt. Geo. Andrews to the Commissioner of Indian Affairs, Arizona City, Nov. 9, 1869, in 234.

'Don't hurry! When you are all ready, call us. Where do you want us to come to fight?[46] Perhaps you mean to run into the brush or up in the mountains. We don't want that; we would like you to stay and fight if you are brave." "Good," they answered, "come over here, it's all level and without brush." So the Chemehuevi all stood lined up there and the Mohave approached them.

184. They began fighting [with arrows] in the morning. At noon, they were tired and rested and some went to drink.[47] Then they began again, and in the afternoon the Chemehuevi ran off up a mountain nearby where all the Chemehuevi women had been sitting watching the battle. The Mohave pursued, caught and dragged down four or five,[48] and killed them. When the sun was nearly down, they returned. Itšiyêre-Өūme had been shot ten times, up on that mountain: he had arrows all over him so he could not sit down.[49] And the Chemehuevi brave man, Apaily-kmaӨ'e, was the same way with arrows all over him so he could not stand; a Chemehuevi carried him off on his back. It was dark when the Mohave came home bringing their many wounded. Some were carried, some were shot in the arm and could walk.

185. There was an agent there then. He said: "I want you Mohave to come and live close to my home: the Chemehuevi are bad."[50] The Mohave who were at Parker told me that he said that. And the Chemehuevi sent word of the fight at Parker to those of their tribe that were still in Chemehuevi Valley, and these all went up into the mountains.

186. Now a hundred Mohave from Mohave Valley[51] went down to Chemehuevi Valley. They found houses, but no one around them. The melons and other crops were ripe so they cut and pulled them and burnt everything and went home.[52]

187. Then a Chemehuevi came with some whites to Fort Mohave,[53] and the Mohave killed him.[54] I saw him, for I was dishwashing for the soldiers then.

188. Now the Chemehuevi heard this. Those of them who had been at Parker were now at Savetpilye, Charleston Peak, west of Eldorado Canyon.[55] Their

---

[46] This sort of sporting-event air characterizes especially the long-range, arrow-shooting battles.

[47] This pausing to rest and to drink is mentioned also for a battle with the Halchidhoma: Kroeber, *Handbook,* p. 800.

[48] Catching hold of enemies and clubbing them dead was the ever-present ultimate aim of Mohave fighting. This incident put them ahead, the score for the previous loss now having been exceeded.

[49] As a result of trying to crowd into close grips, the brave man is thought of as stuck full of arrows, like a pin cushion, by the end of a battle. This idea recurs in Mohave literature.

[50] This sounds like taking sides. Perhaps he said "dangerous" (A.L.K.). Lt. Dodt might well have spoken these words to Mohaves, whom he ordinarily did not consider quite as "hostile" as some other tribes. He reported Chemehuevis' presence on the reservation in his letter of June 5, 1870, in 734, and later petitioned the superintendent to let them stay permanently.

[51] These are from the main part of the tribe still in Mohave Valley, whereas the previous fight was by Mohave from the Parker region. We have seen no report of this expedition, from whites.

[52] Rather purposeless ravaging, as in some other cases, although the Mohave were right enough in guessing that they were about to suffer further Chemehuevi attack.

[53] In what capacity? Why did not the whites protect him? Our records do not say.

[54] See *Weekly Arizona Miner,* July 23 and Aug. 6, 1870. The Mohave who did this was, at least for a time, in the guardhouse.

[55] Savetpilye is the Chemehuevi sacred mountain of creation and flood emergence: Kroeber, *Handbook,* p. 598, and "Notes on California folk-lore. Origin Tradition of the Chemehuevi Indians," *Journal of American Folk-Lore,* 21 (1908), 240-242. The peak, nearly twelve-thousand feet high, is

former brave men being dead, another one rose up, Kwora'āk-uyêyi.[56] He talked war and they all agreed and started.

189. So they came [southeastward], crossed to Cottonwood Island, then into Arizona, and sneaked into the mountains nine miles upriver from Fort Mohave,[57] where they camped without having been seen. Then they went at night to a Mohave settlement four miles down river[58] from the fort, reaching it at daybreak. Some had rifles and pistols, some had bows. The Mohave [there] had no firearms,[59] only bows and clubs; so the Chemehuevi shot and killed many[60] of the few Mohave there. Six Mohave[61] had agreed to try to kill Kwora'āk-uyêyi: "If you catch him, the rest will run off," they said. But the Chemehuevi stayed on and kept shooting; until, in full daylight, a young man, Mat-kwa'êre, leaped out and caught hold of the Chemehuevi chief, and so he[62] was killed; whereupon the Chemehuevi did flee. In such cases the man seized was [thrown] over one's head and held there while others clubbed and dispatched him. In this way the seizer guarded his own head; whereas if he had tried himself to strike his seized foe, the enemy would meanwhile have clubbed him dead.[63]

190. Two other Mohave caught two Chemehuevi who were killed; and though they had no guns, they chased the enemy upriver.[64] I was at the fort working for the Baker when the fleeing Chemehuevi began to come. As the soldiers saw them, they said: "Let's go up and see the fight,"[65] and went up on the

northwest or north-northwest rather than west of Eldorado Canyon (which drains into the Colorado some forty airline miles above Fort Mohave). It is west-southwest of Boulder Dam, and twenty to twenty-five miles nearly west of Las Vegas. The peak is the summit of a massif of no great extent and is not equalled in height as far as the Sierra Madre of Southern California, the Sierra Nevada system, the crests of a few ranges far to the north in Nevada, and the San Francisco Mountains in Arizona. Compared with Savetpilye, mythologically dominant Avikwame of the Mohave is a mere pigmy. The name of Charleston Peak in Chemehuevi-Southern Paiute is Nüvant.

[56] Kworo'āk means old man in Mohave.

[57] This would be in the Black Mountains, a typical basin-and-range type of formation; also presumably near the road from Union Pass, that crosses the range to Harper on the River. The actual direction would be nearer northeast than north.

[58] Unfortunately not named. It might have been Aha-soδape or Qav-kuvaha; but Mohave "miles" are somewhat capricious.

[59] Although there had been a few in the tribe several years before, when they fought the whites: see Episode 9.

[60] This battle took place Oct. 15, 1870: see *Weekly Arizona Miner*, Nov. 12, 1870, closely in accord with the narrator's story; and the Mohave Pete Lambert (Sukulai homar, young plant, grandson of Homose-quahote, elected as Aha macave pipatahon when he was about eight, in 1888; and who told his story many years later): in Kenneth Stewart, "Mohave Warfare," *Southwestern Journal of Anthropology*, 3 (Summer, 1947), 258-259.

[61] Six of those in the attacked settlement? Or had other Mohave begun to come to their rescue? (See n. 64, Episode 12, below: C.B.K.)

[62] The Chemehuevi chief. "Full daylight" refers to the fact that the attack began with the first dawn, so that the fighting had gone on perhaps half an hour, or at most an hour.

[63] This explicit statement agrees with most narrative accounts of the close-in fighting. Normally it would only be a large man who could lift and throw an opponent over his head and hold him there; but men of the river tribes were conspicuously larger than most others in the Southwest.

[64] Sukulai homar (in Stewart, "Mohave Warfare") said that the word had passed southward through the valley, and presumably all able-bodied men came toward the battle on foot, at their best speed. He says that kwanami from the southernmost settlements around Topock never did catch up with the retreating Chemehuevi.

[65] Like the civilians in Episode 8, watching the soldiers chasing the escaped hostages.

mesa. I did not go up.[66] A white man recently told me that this was thirty-seven years ago.[67] No one stopped to look after the dead; all the Mohave were trying to pursue the Chemehuevi. When they got far up on the mesas, the Chemehuevi [turned and] killed two Mohave.[68] Then all the Mohave came home[69] in early afternoon.[70]

191. Then they burned the dead.[71] Twenty-seven Mohave had been shot and badly wounded; ten men were killed, and an old woman. The Chemehuevi leader had a big mass[72] of hair, tied with chickenhawk feathers, and the Mohave scalped him. That night they held the mourning ceremony for warriors[73] for the dead. All the men had been shot, so there were none to run, and girls ran all night carrying the [feathered] sticks [back and forth].[74] I was there, I saw it.

193. The Chemehuevi went home and there was no more fighting for three years.

194. Then some Chemehuevi said: "Let us all quit fighting. We can't beat the Mohave; and we have no home, no place to stay, no food. We travel all the time, get thirsty and hungry, the old men and women die in the desert." So they wanted to stop.[75] And the Mohave went to the government to have them write letters[76] to the Chemehuevi to be friends; and the Chemehuevi came back among them.

EPISODE 13. ACCEPTANCE OF LAW

195. Now when the whites saw that they were peaceful, and the Yavapai and Walapai too, they said they would have irrigating ditches for the Chemehuevi to live by.

---

[66] For once he did not satisfy his curiosity. Perhaps the head baker forbade him.

[67] It was in fact more like thirty-three years earlier.

[68] In the hills the Chemehuevi usually had the advantage, although their party was probably outnumbered by now.

[69] A rather tame ending for a defeat turning into a victory. They probably felt they would suffer losses in crowding the Chemehuevi, now that these were up in the slopes and gullies of the bare Black Mountains.

[70] Six or seven hours may have elapsed, but we do not know how many miles the running fight north and then east traversed, nor how long the Mohave hesitated between pressing the attack further or returning home.

[71] The *Miner* said ten Mohave, and five Chemehuevi; on the reservation, Lt. Dodt, the agent, heard twelve Mohave and three Chemehuevi.

[72] He may just have bunched it; or, again, he may have pencilled it in strands which he wound or coiled in getting ready to fight.

[73] Nyimitš, or hitšpatšk, or nyimitš-ivamk: Kroeber, *Handbook,* p. 750.

[74] This was a piece of brag. Most of the men in the settlement attacked at dawn may have had arrow wounds; but certainly most of the several hundred men of fighting age in the tribe must have been hale (A.L.K.). Of course, we have seen no good indication of how many of the men of fighting age did take part; given the fact that the southernmost Mohave did not arrive in time, it may be that a small proportion of the men carried the brunt of this long fight.

[75] If peace was ever formally made, I do not know it. Chemehuevis had before this been living between La Paz and Yuma, perhaps for some years before this battle. They were living across from the reservation by mid-1869 if not earlier: Agent Tonner to Supt. Bendell, Sept. 20, 1872, in 734, records issuing food to the Chemehuevi at the agency. In his letter of Sept. 25, 1874, he reported having persuaded the Chemehuevi to settle on the western bank of the river: in *Report, Indian Affairs, 1874,* p. 289; see also the *Report* for 1875, p. 552.

[76] The speed with which the almost magical efficacy of written papers becomes accepted among

196. So they went to Hapavese,[1] far below Parker, and there a man named Galloway had charge of all the Indians hired to dig ditches, Chemehuevi and some Mohave too.

197. Now the son of the Chemehuevi chief Apaily-kwaΘ'e[2] crossed to the Arizona side and got drunk there. Recrossing, he came to Galloway's house and wanted to enter. Galloway forbade him, he talked back, Galloway got angry, and when the Chemehuevi would not leave, he shot and killed him. Two or three Chemehuevi who were there saw the shooting, broke into the house, seized Galloway, cut him to pieces with knives, and then chopped his neck with an ax.

198. The Mohave sent word of this from Parker to Fort Mohave. The government[3] said: "You see, if Indians are bad, they get killed."

199. They wanted to make soldiers[4] of the Mohave, and all the Mohave came. Then Asakyêt said: "Wait. Let me first go see the Chemehuevi. Perhaps I can bring in the men that killed Galloway. If they give him up to me good; if not, we can still go and fight."

200. So he went by boat[5] to Parker, and there crossed into California and sent word to the Chemehuevi who by then [had sought refuge] in the mountains, "You are to come down and bring those that killed Galloway." So they came to the river and brought them in. "This man killed Galloway, and this one too." If they had not delivered them, the government would have killed them all, the government said—that is what they were afraid of.[6] "We know now: those who make trouble, we will give them up, and they will be put in the penitentiary. One man starts trouble but it comes on the whole tribe. So we will no longer hide that kind of men." Then the two Chemehuevi were put into San Quentin prison.[7]

201. That was the last fighting; everything was peaceable now. If a Chemehuevi was bad, or a Walapai, or a Mohave, they were turned over to the whites and put into jail. Later, chief Asakyêt had two sons who were cheated by

---

the Indians is really startling.

[1] Hapavese is Blythe, in California (A.L.K.). The man named just below was John P. Calloway, superintendent of "one of the irrigating companies on the Blythe tract": Col. O. B. Willcox, Prescott, Sept. 11, 1880, in *Report, War, 1880,* p. 207.

[2] The same chief mentioned in the twelfth episode. It seems barely possible that this name could be another rendering of that of the chief discussed in several episodes, As-pan-kuh-yah as Brady put it. The version of this series of incidents given by Chooksa homar closely resembles that of Indian Agent Henry R. Mallory, in his letter to the Commissioner of Indian Affairs, from the River Reservation, March 31, 1880, in Colorado River Reservation, Letters to Commissioner, 1879-1917, Federal Records Center, Bell, California, and in other sources cited in Discussions, below.

[3] Lt.-Col. La Motte, then commanding Fort Mohave?

[4] I do not know whether this rally of Mohaves by U.S. authorities occurred at Fort Mohave, or on the reservation, or whether it did occur at all. See Discussions, below.

[5] By steamboat, we assume. He may already have been leader of the Fort Mojave Indian police, as he was in later years. That he did, or at least four leading Mohave did, come down from the fort, is attested by sources cited in Discussions, below (C.B.K.).

[6] By that time the army had arrived in force, several companies of soldiers and some from as far away as San Francisco.

[7] This was, of course, a lesson not readily learned by tribes with only rudiments of political organization and sanction. The Walapai were taught it by an army officer who gave orders to have a criminal's hand brought him; whereupon his friends and relatives ambushed and shot him to save themselves; and, when some of their less informed tribesmen questioned this way of doing, told them that ways had been changed by the Americans: see *Walapai Ethnography,* (Menasha, Wis., 1935), p. 214 (A.L.K.).

a white man and killed him. Asakyêt himself gave them up.[8] They were sent to San Quentin and one of them died there. So there was no more fighting.

[8] On this flat note of achieved virtuousness our story ends. At any rate there was peace (A.L.K.). See plate 6, picturing a group gathered together on account of this incident, in 1887.

CHAPTER 3

DISCUSSIONS

Episode 1. War with the Cocopa: Captives

THIS EPISODE deals with events and persons well known to written history, although no exact date can be given. Part of the uncertainty as to details has to do with the second-hand nature of the narrative. The narrator, perhaps eight or ten years of age when these events transpired, must have heard this story in later years from Mohave participants like Yara tav whom he knew personally. For our purposes, there has been a scarcity of reports by white men. There were no Indian agents in Yuma or the vicinity in the early 1850s, and I have not found useful army records. For instance, there seems to be no report of the Mohaves' meeting with the commandant of Fort Yuma at which time "papers" were issued to the five Mohave chiefs. The fact that papers were issued seems beyond question, since Lieutenant Amiel Whipple saw two such documents in the hands of Mohave in 1854. One of the men holding these documents must have been Tapaikunehe, who is mentioned here by the Mohave narrator.

To put this Mohave-Quechan raid on the Cocopa in some perspective, it was one of the last campaigns in what had been a traditional hostility going back into the eighteenth century or before, as Jack Forbes has shown.[1] The Quechan and Mohave tended to raid, and the Quechan to be raided by, other tribes of whom the Cocopa were one. These hostilities usually took the form of hit-and-run raids, or, where safe enough to do it, extermination of a whole village population. They did not come to an end when the Gila Trail filled up with forty-niners rushing to California, or when a United States Army post was placed at Yuma. Nor did such raiding cease even during the confusing period of hostilities between Indians and whites during the early 1850s. We do not know when the last of these intertribal raids occurred, but the Cocopa were hoping to draw the Maricopa into an attack against the Yuma in 1854, and the Quechans then expected to be attacked. And, in 1856 Pascual, the leader of the Quechans, still looked for a Cocopa raid.[2]

---

[1] Forbes, *Warriors of the Colorado* (Norman, Okla., 1965), pp. 74 ff., esp. 80-81, as to the general affinities within two rough alignments of tribes in the Southwest, and hostilities between tribes, across such lines of affinity: see also A. L. Kroeber, *Handbook of the Indians of California* (Washington, D.C., 1925), p. 596, and Forbes, pp. 289-292, for specific Cocopa-Quechan hostilities in the 1830s and 1840s. There were no "alliances" or "leagues" as whites understand these matters, simply habits of teaming with some warriors of a given tribe to raid another tribe—with little or no economic motive as regards the Mohave. Statements to the effect that a main motive for Mohave war was economic, for captives to be made slaves, are not persuasive since the raids occurred only infrequently and very few captives were taken home from them.

[2] For 1854, Julius Froebel, *Seven Years' Travel* . . . (London, 1859), p. 524, who met Cocopas en route to the Pimas in late July; for the Quechans in 1854 and 1856, letters of commandants of Fort Yuma, Capt. Geo. H. Thomas, Aug. 8, 1854, and Capt. Martin Burke, Jan. 3, 1856, both in Fort Yuma, B-4 and T-13, in 393.

So, there were raids, counter-raids, and ambushes by Cocopa and Quechan on each other at various times from 1851 to 1854, and the Mohave were called in and took part more than once. Our question is: Which raid is the narrator discussing, and when did it occur?

By an incomplete process of elimination I suspect that this attack took place during early 1854, although there is no reliable witness. If the raid had come before July 1853, it would have been noticed in a report made by the commandant of Fort Yuma, Captain Samuel P. Heintzelman,[3] who was then seeking answers to all sorts of questions about Indians, and notably the Mohave of whom he knew little. Heintzelman had a taste for detail, and a manifest desire to demonstrate to his superiors his success in overawing and organizing the nearby natives. And, up until late 1853 his active subaltern, Lieutenant "Fighting Tom" Sweeny, kept a good diary[4] and included just such events as the narrator describes here.

Perhaps the best hint we now have as to the date of this raid comes indirectly from a white girl, Olive Oatman, who was then captive among the Mohave. In a book put together from her story by her sponsor, Royal Stratton, she remembered that in 1854 there had been two Cocopa women captives with the Mohave. Later that year the Mohave went on a big raid, with the Yuma against the Cocopa, and brought back five more Cocopa women as captives.[5]

To get at this in another way, I know of no circumstantial accounts of any Mohave-Yuma raid on the Cocopa after 1854. After long delay because of the Yumas' nervousness, Captain George H. Thomas was able to bring about a formal peace treaty between leaders of the two tribes, on January 24, 1855.[6] But whether this treaty was respected or not, we do not know; nor do we know whether this was the ceremony mentioned at the end of this episode.

Aside from dating and verifying the incident, there is a great deal of interest in this first episode. We see graphic indications that traditional conduct was mixing with adaptations to the presence and desires of the whites. This same sort of evidence of acculturation will be seen in most of the episodes that follow. This particular campaign was in a traditional framework, both as to alliance with the Quechan, the brevity of the attack itself and its limited objectives, its leadership by a few professional warriors (kwanami), and its outcome in general good

---

[3] Report of July 15, 1853, printed as document 76 in 34 Congress 3 Session, vol. 9 (Washington, D.C., 1857), pp. 34 ff.

[4] *Journal of Lt. Thomas W. Sweeny, 1849-1853,* ed. Arthur Woodward (Los Angeles, 1953); and the ms. diary and other Sweeny papers in the Huntington Library, San Marino, California.

[5] Royal B. Stratton, *Captivity of the Oatman Girls* . . . 3rd. ed., 1858: reprinted, edited by Lindley Bynum, as *Life Among the Indians* (San Francisco, 1935). Stratton says this raid occurred some time during or after spring, 1854. The *Yuma Arizona Sentinel,* May 4, 1878, stated that a raid yielding five Cocopa captives occurred some time after September 1853. Sweeny reported the Mohave, along with Chemehuevi and Yavapai, wasting Cocopa crops in mid-September 1853: *Journal,* pp. 211-212. Heintzelman's letter of March 16, 1854, says that this three-tribal descent on the Cocopa occurred "last summer": see Fort Yuma, in 393. The *Los Angeles Times,* April 19, 1856, mentioned a Mohave-Yuma attack on the Cocopa "last year," yielding "several prisoners."

[6] Articles of Agreement entered into between the Captains of the Cuchanos or Yumas and the Captains of the Cocopas . . . .: Fort Yuma, in 393. See also Report of Lt. N. Michler, in *United States and Mexican Boundary Survey,* document 135 in 34 Congress 1 Session 1856, part I (Washington, D.C., 1857), pp. 107-108; he was there at the time. His list of signers is not complete.

feelings and some slaves to take home. But at every step we see that this episode did not occur in an aboriginal world. The Mohave stop over at Fort Yuma for an arrangement with the commandant, and their spokesman is not the tribal head chief, Homose-quahote—even though he was helping to lead the war party—but another subordinate chief, Yara tav.

By that time Yara tav had already made that cautious assessment of the power of the white Americans which became notable in his career among Indians and whites in western Arizona. He was gaining status by his initiative in seeking out the white Americans and conferring with them. In the brief quotations in the text we dimly see the intratribal negotiator at work. Later, he would broaden the scope of his relationships and his influence with the whites and tribes other than his own.

Finally, this first episode raises questions about the narrator's viewpoint, and about the method used in recording what he said in 1903. Toward the end one begins to wonder whether the version we have here is that of Yara tav, rendered quite some time after the facts. There could be some self-justification in the viewpoint expressed here, with an eye to the United States Army invasion of Mohave Valley that occurred a few years later.

More importantly, the narrator is of course delivering a heavily selective account. At this distance it is impossible to say whether he is so selective because this outline of events is all he ever knew, or whether Chooksa homar himself decided what to tell and what to omit. Did he say everything he had heard about these events? We will never know, and I see no means of deducing an answer to the question.

Most importantly, by 1903 the narrator had lived through the apprehensive and confusing early years of domination by the whites, including some very disturbing events attendant upon the shift of control from army to Interior Department about 1890 and thereafter. His vocabulary, and whole quotations he gives here, may well be placed as they are, and phrased as they are, because it was a white man who was listening and recording.

The use of "bad" and "good" stands out, and will be found in later episodes. A close reading of some of the short speeches by Indians gives a strong impression that part of a quotation may be reportage, put along with a moralistic sentiment thought to be necessary in the presence of the white listener. The whole speech by the kwohota in paragraph 16 may be such a pious fabrication.

The listener, A. L. Kroeber, expected something like this. He was working through a translator, Quichnyailk, a Mohave whose intelligence and alertness Kroeber came deeply to respect. But there was little time to mine into the subtleties or to harry the narrator for restatements of what he was saying. Kroeber seems to have confined his requests for clarification to specific cultural items; and he depended upon Quichnyailk to get amplifications, when the original statement in Mohave seemed equivocal to the interpreter. Likewise, at the time Kroeber had not read the white man's histories or published documents then available, so he was not fully equipped to ask leading questions that might have led to a deepening of historical understandings.

Finally, as for the background in published history and unpublished manuscripts that could elucidate this episode, we may well have missed something important among the various kinds of United States Army records now on deposit in the National Archives at Washington, D.C. Strangely enough, we did not find many published memoirs or newspaper items, although Fort Yuma was visited by so many travelers and officials during the 1850s. Some of this can be accounted for by the then early stage of white occupation, and by Yuma's disfavored and isolated locale so far as whites were concerned; and, by destruction of army records in repeated fires at Fort Yuma. Still, I hope someone will soon turn up the United States Army version of the paper-granting ceremony, perhaps even with a transcript of the commandant's remarks at the time.

EPISODE 2. FIRST CONFLICT WITH AMERICANS

This episode starkly and no doubt accurately pictures the confusion and doubt within the Mohave mind as white settlement drew closer, as white visitors came more often, and as such inexplicable novelties as the gun, the camel, and the steamboat, had to be accepted as part of their world. Not that these living Mohave were seeing the white man for the first time, as was generally supposed by so many of the whites themselves and is still assumed by some historians. While we cannot provide anything like a complete roster of all those white men who had moved through Mohave country during the thirty years before the coming of this emigrant train, it is obvious that many white men had come, some in peace and some suddenly in war.

In the 1820s and 1830s there were many scrapes with larger or smaller beaver-hunting brigades. To mention but one, Peter Skene Ogden's thirty trappers with their single-shot muskets, being met derisively and roughly handled by the Mohave in 1830, killed twenty-six and moved on.[7] Jedediah Smith had very different reception on his two visits to Mohave Valley, welcomed one time and ambushed the next, and the difference probably was that between his two visits a sizeable trapping party had come by and thoroughly savaged the Mohave men and women. Even where hostilities did not strike the Mohave directly, they heard of whites attacking other tribes, all over the desert and mountain Southwest. They heard of events such as Felix Aubry's bitter hostilities with the neighboring Walapai in 1853-1854.[8] In fact, Aubry may have crossed Mojave Valley itself.

Worse yet for the Mojave, they saw the white man's settlements coming closer and bringing conflict with them. From the north, the missionaries of the Church of Jesus Christ of Latter-Day Saints came among the Mojave in 1857 but were much more closely associated with the Paiute, not close friends of the Mojaves. To the south, steady travel by whites on the Gila Trail for years was now surmounted by the establishment of Fort Yuma and the formal cowing of the

[7] Leroy R. Hafen and Ann W. Hafen, *The Old Spanish Trail* (Glendale, Calif., 1854), pp. 137-139, and sources they cite.
[8] Walker D. Wyman, "F. X. Aubry: Santa Fe Freighter, Pathfinder, and Explorer," *New Mexico Historical Review*, 7 (Jan., 1932), 1-32, appending two brief journals of trips; and Ralph B. Bieber, ed., *Exploring Southwestern Trails, 1846-1853* (Glendale, Calif., 1938), including Aubry's 1853 journal.

Quechan nation, close friends of the Mojaves. To Mojave Valley itself had come a series of overland United States government explorers, during the 1850s and very recently the steamboat ascents of the Colorado by Lieutenant James L. White, and Lieutenant Joseph C. Ives, in 1857-1858, and Lieutenant Edward F. Beale's several passages through Mohave country during the same period of time.

Worst of all (as Henry Dobyns has suggested to us) this Rose-Hedgpeth party of 1858 was the very first to bring white women and children through Mojave Valley. The Mohave narrator has told us how concerned were the Indians that this might be a colonizing expedition. The emigrant L. J. Rose tells the same story: three times, on two days the travelers spent in the river bottom before being attacked, they were approached by different groups of Indians all asking the same question: Do you mean to settle here? One of the chiefs, upon hearing that California was the promised land, seemed not to believe that these whites did mean to move on.[9]

So the Indians were not only divided among themselves as to how to deal with the emigrants but were also very apprehensive. For their part the emigrant party was almost incredibly naive and unready for this meeting with a formidable Indian nation, not met casually as a small hunting party on some trail but in large numbers in their own home villages. The whites, desperate for water, pushed too hard to reach the river and spent their first half-day there in collapse and exhaustion, passive while the Indians laughingly "drove off our cattle without opposition," cooked the meat in plain sight, mauled the women and laughed in the faces of men who intervened. The hired leader of the party, Alpha Brown, was overly busy in bringing water for the people and the stock, and two days later was still engrossed in necessary work, preparing for the river crossing. He was not watchful, nor was the experienced guide José M. Saavedra whom the army authorities at Albuquerque had forced this party to engage, before permitting them to go on. Saavedra had been this way before but was perhaps not closely enough attuned to the meanings of Indian comings and goings. On the third day with Mohave and Chemehuevi gathering in large numbers, many swimming the stream from the west bank, he finally warned that the Mojave were acting "suspiciously."[10] The bill for all this was something like nine whites killed and another sixteen wounded.

Although the whites held the Indians at bay with gunfire, they lost almost all the stock and made their way back up the trail with but two wagons and perhaps three dozen of the more than four hundred cattle and horses they had brought to the Colorado. Many of these people would have died, on the hard push back to Albuquerque, but for their meeting two more emigrant trains not far back along the trail, and but for timely help from the United States Army in reaching them with food and other assistance.

This event sealed the fate of the Mohave as an independent people. It furnished just that core of new information which sharpened the impression

---

[9] See pp. 310-311 in R. G. Cleland, *The Cattle on a Thousand Hills* (San Marino, Calif., 1941), as cited above.

[10] Ibid., p. 311. Brown was getting together rafts for crossing the cattle. Mr. Rose sent word to have the cattle brought closer to camp, because of the threatening look of things. Brown was killed on the way back with the stock, some three to five hours later.

white men had had of the Mohave up to that time. As seen in newspapers, memoirs, accounts of travelers, and military correspondence from New Mexico on through to Los Angeles and San Francisco, that feeling was a compound of several elements. There was ignorance of the Aha macave; half-remembered horror stories of conflict with some trapping expedition; and recent if groundless suspicion that the Mohave must have been implicated in local Indian uprisings against the whites since 1850, like the one led by Antonio Garra in 1851 or the alliance against the whites planned by Juan Antonio in 1855. At a deeper level was a general, although not universal, assumption on the part of white Americans of that day, to the effect that the Indian's primitive way was passing. Now that the flare of civilization's torch had appeared before their eyes, the red men and their unfit cultures would shrivel and fade away. Many white Americans felt that this process needed no acceleration by war: let the Indian live quietly by the side of the emigrant trail, and he will soon disappear. But here was a tribe that would resist its doom, and the U.S. government moved quickly to crush such resistance.

As for observation of the events of this incident with the emigrant train, it appears that Chooksa homar has compressed three days' events into two. He seems to have come late to the scene, as upon a later occasion to be found in another episode in this narrative. When he arrived, women and children were still straggling in from the trail, some of the party having pushed on more rapidly and arrived the day before.

Episode 3. Peace Made with the Maricopa

Some of the questions raised here are: When did Yara tav make this trip to the Gila River? And, why at that very time? Did all this happen as related in this narrative, or are we seeing only fragments of some larger series of events of which Chooksa homar does not speak? As one might expect, finding answers to one or two of these questions does depend somewhat upon already having answers to one or two others. We have not found our way into this network of proof at any one point with such assurance as to be able to offer a reliable interpretation. What we have done instead is to make some assumptions and, going from these to a search for facts, to arrive at an interpretation of this episode in light of those facts. The objective has been to date the episode and to derive its meaning.

First, we assume it very unlikely that Yara tav would have made any such trip to the Maricopa at the time suggested in the narrative—just after the 1858 attack on the emigrant train. Knowing the dates of the episodes just before and just after this one, we know that about four months intervened between them: from the end of August 1858 until January 1859. This leaves ample time for Yara tav to have carried out such a peace mission as is described here. But we assume that Yara tav would have been otherwise occupied, at home in Mohave Valley listening to and talking with everyone, as was his habit at times of danger and decision. My own guess is that if he traveled at all during these four months, it would have been back down to Yuma, to find out what the white soldiers had to say, and what they would do, in light of the disaster to the Rose party.

Alternatively, Yara tav might have received news of that attack while he was still at Yuma, hearing it from the ever-active "Indian expresses" that moved up and down the river constantly. He might have stayed near the United States Army detachment for a time, then would have returned by slow stages, stopping to talk again wherever he encountered some Mojave family or small village settlement of people at work in the river lowlands or moving about gathering food.

Furthermore, we assume that there was no discernible reason for a trip to the Maricopa, during the fall of 1859 or for some years afterward. After the attack on the Cocopa, yes, it would have made sense to go personally, to reestablish friendly relations with Pima and Maricopa if possible, and—most of all—to discover whether these Gila River tribes were inclined to accept the army's standing invitation to them to come down and settle near Yuma, so as to overawe the Quechans there. But in 1859 we see no reason for full-dress diplomacy; and I assume that Yara tav's public acts invariably had some careful planning behind them and were carefully timed to achieve success and full effect.

Beginning in late 1861 and from then on, the picture changed radically and Indian diplomacy was needed as never before in behalf of the safety of the Mohave. There was a new intensity in whites' activities, which involved a much more pervasive presence in western Arizona and new and complex processes for the Mojave to deal with. Mining discoveries were made along the Colorado River and now attracted great attention, bringing the vanguard of what soon became an invasion by thousands of would-be miners. The Civil War brought Confederate troops into Arizona, westward from Tucson for a short time, and then the United States Army response soon began to remake the picture of white settlement in southern Arizona, with implications for Indians north of the Gila. And when Colonel Joseph R. West arrived at Fort Yuma in November 1861, he found that the Quechans "were at war" still with the Pima and Maricopa.[11]

In Yara tav's homeland, the army eventually reopened Fort Mojave which had stood empty since the spring of 1861. There also came to be federal policies that sought to enlist the support of some Arizona tribes against the Apache menace on one hand and against the Paiute on the other. A territorial government was established in Arizona early in 1864, and it added a strident voice to the problems already existing for both whites and Indians. Indian agencies were established—Herman Ehrenberg took up his duties at La Paz on the Colorado River on July 1, 1863—and soon there was the prospect of a reservation of arable land for the Mohave and other nearby tribes to be established on the Colorado in 1865.

Not only did the territory begin to fill up with settlements of white people and their confusing and overlapping jurisdictional and personal allegiances. More dangerous for the Indians, Arizona was now the target of small, wandering parties of whites, heavily armed, with no idea how to find precious metal ore, without machines to grind it down, and with no jobs to fall back on if mining should fail them. Many were unable to find steady employment; they were suspicious of each other, federal or "secesh"; and they were fearful and resentful

---

[11] William A. Keleher, *Turmoil in New Mexico, 1846-1868* (Santa Fe, N.M., 1952), p. 225.

at the presence of the Indian behind every other hill. It was this presence of a new kind of white man, beginning in Arizona in 1862 and 1863, that was later described by one of them as "a powerful and armed idleness";[12] and it made the Indian's life suddenly much more dangerous.

These white men were camping at the springs upon which the Indians depended for life. They crossed the country in ever increasing numbers, cutting across the routes the Indians were following to gather mescal or mesquite here and saguaro there, to leave a small crop in the ground at another place, or to visit where the pine nuts were come to their time of ripening. Although it would be difficult to prove, my own assumption is that from the early 1860s onward one difficulty between whites and Indians was in just this, the very unexpectedness and unpredictableness of their meetings, as the immigrant scrabbled in a canyon for gold while the native American came into view along one of the mountain trails.

If Yara tav did not go to the Maricopa in 1859, then when and why would he have gone at any other date? I assume that he went in 1863, and that he was providing in advance against any danger of Maricopa attack against the Mohave, backed by the powder and ball and steel of the whites. Further, I suppose that Yara tav was also trying to shelter some bands of Western Yavapai, who spent some time each year in southern Mohave lands where they would visit and gather the mesquite bean alongside their friends. And I assume that the need for an understanding with the Maricopa was quite new, growing out of the conditions we have just discussed. For generations before 1862 no such diplomatic mission would have been thought of. Relations with the Pima and Maricopa were simple enough: these tribes were the targets for the large-scale, formal war expeditions launched by the Mohave, alone or with Quechan and Yavapai allies. And this was a feature of Mohave warfare that was fortunate enough for them, since the return raids from the Gila seem all to have gone against the Yuma, not into Mohave country.

But by 1862 and even more in 1863, there was urgent need to remake this relationship. The whites and Pima-Maricopa had fallen into friendly relationship; they had never fought so much as an acquaintance battle to begin with. Now there were unmistakable efforts to use Gila River Indians as volunteers against nearby tribes whom the whites might classify as "hostile." Just when this practice began, I do not know, but the whites brought the idea with them from earlier experiences, and the custom was establishing in Arizona by early 1863.[13]

---

[12] Daniel Conner, *Joseph Reddeford Walker and the Arizona Adventure* (Norman, Okla., 1956), p. 156.

[13] Keleher, *Turmoil in New Mexico,* p. 241, shows that Brig. Gen. Jas. H. Carleton, commanding the California Column of volunteer federal troops pushing through Arizona early in 1862, asked higher authority to furnish the Pimas one hundred stand of old percussion muskets, cartridges, and bullet molds. I think the matter dragged for quite a while before the Pima received arms. Charles Poston, appointed Superintendent of Indian Affairs for Arizona in March 1863 was early in this field: "I organized a company of Pima and Maricopas as scouts. They had recently received arms and ammunition from the Government . . .": *Building a State in Apache Land* (Tempe, Arizona, 1963: orig. publ. in July-Oct. numbers of *Overland Monthly,* 1894), p. 118. See *War of the Rebellion,* 50, pt. 2 (Washington, D.C., 1897), pp. 405-406, for Col. David Fergusson's letter, Tucson, April 17, 1863, ordering one hundred stand of old arms, ammunition, and other items, to the Pima villages on what he thought of as "loan," while Pimas used them against Apaches. See his orders to Capt. T. T. Tidball, Tucson, May 2, 1863, for a twelve-day raid against Apaches, with twenty-five picked

As early as January 1860, Jack Swilling took Maricopa with him as he carried fire and sword from the Gila up into Yavapai country.[14]

By 1863, what this meant was that the United States Army command in the Southwest would stage campaigns against the Apache as soon as possible to do it and were only restrained by the feeling that the Confederate States of America might still make another invasion of New Mexico and Arizona. In May 1863, it was still believed that the Confederates were coming back.[15]

This was not the worst of it from a Mohave's viewpoint. In the traditional alternation of raids against one another the Mohave, Yuma, and Yavapai had made the latest attack, in 1857, and they might now expect to be raided by the Maricopa in return. If I am right about Yara tav—that he was quite able to work across the line that lay between traditional custom and new conditions of life—it does seem reasonable for him to have sought a meeting with Juan Chivaria at any time during 1863. And there are sources that come close to saying that he did.

If we seek for records of a peace meeting between Mohave and Maricopa in 1863, the question is not: Was there one? but, Were there two? For it is clear that Superintendent Poston, entering upon his new tasks in the grand manner, held a general peace conference at Fort Yuma in early April 1863. He was new enough to the work to be vague about which Indians were represented, and somehow none of the host tribe, the Quechans, autographed the agreement. But those who did sign were, all of them, already identified by the whites as the individuals who could speak for their tribes in relations with the white man: Yara tav for Mojaves, Juan Chivaria for Maricopas and Antonio Azul for the Pima; Ah-pan-kuh-ya of the Chemehuevi, and Quashackama who was thought to be "head chief" of the Yavapai.[16]

Briefly stated, the treaty bound each tribe to help the others in war against the Apache; to help to bring in any Indian who acted against an "American"; forbade any of these tribes to negotiate separate treaties with Apaches, unless all these tribes should agree to do so. The fourth article specifies particular care toward miners "in lonely and isolated places in small parties," and reminds these tribes that they, "being chiefly an agricultural and stock raising population," should conclude to protect the "Americans" against all acts to the injury of such Americans, by any member of any of these tribes. The final provision is of most interest here, for it speaks of "obliterating" any thought of retaliation against each other for any reason of past "difficulties" between tribes. This was, at least in part, what Yara tav wanted when he went to see Juan Chivaria.

---

soldiers, ten "American citizens" and thirty-two Mexicans "With about 20 Papagos from San Xavier [outskirts of Tucson, today] and their Governor," and "Nine tame Apaches will be Sent with you as Spies and guides": Records of the War Department, 10th Military District, vol. 85: Tucson, Post Letters, 1862-1863, USNA. Conner, p. 74, passing through the Pima villages at about that time, said that the "government was furnishing them with farming implements and condemned muskets."

[14] Albert H. Schroeder, *A Study of Yavapai History,* 1 (3 parts, mimeographed: Santa Fe, N.M., 1959), pp. 84-85.

[15] Keleher, *Turmoil in New Mexico,* p. 330, and sources he cites. Keleher's account is valuable background for Arizona events of that day.

[16] See a copy in 734. When this "treaty" arrived in Washington, D.C., the answer was chilling: "You are not empowered to make treaties except when specially empowered to do so": Wm. P. Dole, Commissioner of Indian Affairs, to Poston, Washington D.C., July 16, 1863, in Records of the Office of Indian Affairs, Letters Sent, 1863-1864, USNA.

Was there any other such peace conference in Arizona in 1863? This is a question that has so far not yielded to research, but that has accumulated some tantalizing indications. I have tried to "fix" a few of the discrete incidents in Chooksa homar's narrative—the visit to Sacatón, Agua Caliente, and Tucson—I have tried to work out itineraries for Yara tav and for another likely participant, the white trapper Pauline Weaver, from 1861 through 1864. I have scraped for sources that might, even tangentially, show up firm corroboration of this second peace treaty, or a convincing disqualification of it.

First, to try to bring to the surface Pauline Weaver's role in events around Agua Caliente, Arizona Territory, in 1863. He was then in his mid-sixties and like many old trappers had turned to odd jobs of guiding and scouting. Insofar as Arthur Woodward can trace his movements, Weaver had sold out his land at San Gorgonio in Southern California in 1853 and had moved about, mostly in Arizona after 1864, until his death in 1867.[17] Woodward also feels that Yara tav was accompanied to this peace meeting by John Moss, who later sponsored Yara tav on a trip to San Francisco, New York, and Washington, D.C. No doubt Moss's interest in Yara tav related to Moss's association with a high-powered group of capitalists who intended to make very important mining investments along the upper Colorado, just north of Fort Mohave and in other locations nearby.[18]

That Weaver had turned from his earlier Indian-killing career to intermittent peace efforts among the Indians is clear enough. Among others the Yavapai Michael Burns attested to this.[19] And one of the earliest white immigrants into north-central Arizona, Charlie Genung, stoutly maintained that Weaver had made an Indian treaty in June 1863, at Agua Caliente. Weaver had indeed been all over Arizona recently, guiding the first company of California Volunteers that distantly followed the retreating Confederates eastward from Fort Yuma in March-April 1862.[20] He had earlier made a mining discovery near the site of La Paz on the Colorado. Now, drifting back to Yuma, he met Genung and others to guide them into northeastern Arizona in early 1863.[21]

[17] "Pauline Weaver of the Restless Feet," *Desert Magazine,* 2 (March, 1938), 4-6, and *Feud on the Colorado,* (Los Angeles, Calif., 1955), pp. 83-84, probably resting on Sharlot Hall, *First Citizen of Prescott, Pauline Weaver* (Prescott, Ariz., 1929), pp. 7, 20, who in turn probably used the Genung manuscripts to back her conclusion that there was a second peace treaty in 1863. See Charlie Genung, "About My Experiences with the Colorado Indian Reservation and the Apaches," ms. in Sharlot Hall Museum, Prescott. Genung flatly stated that the treaty among Pima, Maricopa, Yuma, and Mohave, "was made near the Agua Caliente on the Gila River in June, 1863." See also his "How He Became a Hassayamper," 1863, ibid.
[18] As seen in papers in the Huntington Library, San Marino, Calif., to which W. H. Hutchinson kindly drew my attention.
[19] His brief narrative is in T. E. Farish, *History of Arizona* (8 vols., Phoenix, Ariz., 1915-1918), 3 pp. 288-300: see p. 298. He was a Northeastern Yavapai born about 1864, taken by U.S. soldiers in 1872 and raised by Capt. James Burns, U.S.A. Later he served as a most effective communicant with Prof. Edward Gifford.
[20] George Washington Oaks, *Man of the West: Reminiscences of... 1840-1917* ...ed. Arthur Woodward (Tucson, Ariz., 1956).
[21] Genung, in *Prescott Evening Courier,* May 20, 1911, says he left San Francisco July 27, 1863, too late for our interpretation here. But others involved set these dates much earlier: Conner (see n. 25 just below) gives dates of public record showing that Genung must have left California months earlier than he says. A. H. Peeples (this Genung-Weaver group being known as the Peeples Party) later

Weaver later claimed back salary, "To Services as Indian Agent in Arizona in the absence of any authorized official in the Government, engaged in preserving peace with the Indian tribes, making a Treaty of Peace with the Americans and the following tribes, viz., Yumas, Maricopas, Pimas, Papagos, Chemihuevis, Hualpais by which they made an alliance against the Apaches all of which resulted in the discovery and occupation of the Mines, say from 1 January 1863 to the 30 June 1864 . . . ."[22]

All this makes it seem that there was but one treaty, done at Fort Yuma in April. Still, the Halchidhoma, Kutox, recalled that Pengiwtcsa (Beaver Eater), an American trapper living near Sacatón, "brought the Mohave to them to make peace in 1863."[23] And Weaver certainly was at the Pima Villages on March 5, 1863, and for some time afterward.[24] So, Weaver was in the neighborhood of Sacatón during mid-1863, and both the white man Genung and the Maricopa Kutox speak of a treaty made in that vicinity, that year.

Yara tav was also there. Daniel Conner was entering the region in early 1863 in the "Walker Party" seeking after mining opportunities, with the famous Joseph R. Walker as their guide. As nearly as I can estimate dates in Conner's account, his party met Yara tav just after turning north from the Gila toward the Hassayampa, at some time between April 23 and 29. Then Yara tav left the party, on one of the days between April 29 and May 5.[25] The Walker Party, after locating claims, went on down from the Hassayampa to buy food, and there in the desert they met Weaver, escorting the Peeples Party, still west of the Pima villages.[26] It is still harder to estimate the date of this meeting. Conner says it was in June 1863, "but we knew not what day of the month it was and we really dated our records as of that month at a venture." My guess is that they met Weaver between May 28 and mid-June 1863. Finally, it is clear that Weaver and his party did arrive on the Hassayampa in time to establish land claims in July.[27]

recalled that they found Weaver at Fort Yuma "just then . . . completing a treaty of peace between the Pimas and Maricopa and the Mohaves, being implicitly trusted as an arbitrator." So the Peeples Party with Weaver as guide was mustering at Yuma in early April 1863.

[22] One of a file in 234; this document was done at La Paz, June 30, 1864. And for verification of his services Weaver referred the U.S. government to the "Books of the Ajutant's Office at Ft. Yuma, on Indian Treaties," for facts "in regard to my transaction with the different Indian Tribes": in another document, ibid., written to Charles Poston, La Paz, May 6, 1864. I am told that one fire after another finally made away with the adjutant's files of Fort Yuma.

[23] Leslie Spier, *Yuman Tribes of the Gila River* (Chicago, 1933), pp. 45, 161, 174, who talked with Kutox (born at Sacatón ca. 1847) in 1929-1930. Spier also talked with a Kaveltcadom-Kohuana living in this same mixed "Maricopa" community, who had only started his calendar stick in 1873-1874 but who had memorized events earlier than that, and showed a record for 1863-1864: "Made a peace treaty with the Yavapai:" ibid., p. 140.

[24] Letters of Capt. Wm. French, commanding at Tucson, dated June 21 and Aug. 11, 1863, in Tucson, Post Letters, 1862-1863, in 393. Weaver initiated correspondence March 5, and it is clear from French's note of Aug. 11 that Weaver had answered French's of June 21, from the Pima villages.

[25] Conner, pp. 74-91, by working back from a firm date corresponding with the eighteenth day of the trip (May 10, 1863), a day when they inscribed various documents which became public record in Yavapai County: the editors of Conner's account, Donald Berthrong and Odessa Davenport, cite to these documents.

[26] Conner, p. 104.

[27] Weaver's preemption claim to a quarter section at what became known as Walnut Grove, a claim he stated that he made in July 1863: copy in Sharlot Hall Museum, Prescott, Arizona.

This all seems to leave open the possibility that Yara tav went on to the Maricopa villages (Maricopa Wells, in the whites' parlance), and there met Pauline Weaver as well as Juan Chivaria and other Maricopa. And if they met there at that time, it is quite possible that an army officer could have been there. Certainly there was a white captain at Tucson at that time.[28]

If this Agua Caliente meeting did occur, and if both Yara tav and Weaver were there, it could have come late in 1863 but not so easily as earlier in the year. By mid-June Yara tav was starting out on a two-weeks' trip west of Fort Mohave, guiding some white men; and in mid-September he began again the long foot trip from Fort Mohave to Fort Yuma, as official bearer of an urgent piece of army correspondence.[29] Presumably he left the Colorado River in November, starting the long trip to the eastern United States from which he would only return in late May 1864. In Chooksa homar's narrative we see Yara tav returning from his trip to the Maricopa, arriving back at his home on the east side of Mohave Valley, where he had been living in 1860 as Peter Brady then reported. Since Yara tav left this original home in 1865,[30] moving south out of Mohave Valley not to return again to live there, the trip to the Maricopa must have been undertaken no later than 1865.

Finally, if it seems unlikely that Yara tav would have felt the need for a direct understanding with the Maricopa, we should remember that during 1862 and the early months of 1863 he had no army protectors at home in Mohave Valley. The fort had been unoccupied for two years and troops returned to it only on May 19, 1863.[31]

EPISODE 4. SECOND CONFLICT WITH THE AMERICANS

This encounter with S. A. Bishop's party, on its way to supply Lieutenant E. F. Beale's reconnoitering and road-making party upon its arrival at the Colorado

---

[28] And the Tucson post would have looked small. Its commander had few troops on hand even though managing the relay of the California Column at that time. Capt. Whitlock reported only fifty men and three officers, on March 23; on June 27 Capt. French had but thirty-two enlisted and two other officers beside himself: Tucson Post Letters, in 393. I imagine that Yara tav stopped outside the town, in any case.

Gen. Carleton's troops had occupied Tucson May 19, 1862 (Tucson post return, May 31, 1862, in 617) and thereafter a great many small military units did pass through or stay over at Sacatón, going to buy wheat at the Pima villages and on other errands, or carrying the weekly army mail. As examples: Capt. Whitlock to Lt. G. A. Burkett, ordering him to go to the villages and stay to get as much grain as possible: Tucson, March 17, 1863, in Tucson Post Letters, 1862-1863, in 393. The Headquarters Group of 5th Regiment of Infantry, California Volunteers, was en route from near Yuma to Tucson May 1-14, 1863: in Records of the War Department, Compiled Records Showing Service of Military Units in Volunteer Union Organization: California: Regimental Returns, 5th Regiment of Infantry, USNA. But I have seen no army reports of any meeting with Indians at Sacatón.

[29] *Alta California,* Aug. 2, 1863 [transcript in Arizona Pioneers' Historical Society] and Capt. J. Ives Fitch to Commandant of Fort Yuma, Fort Mohave, Sept. 19, 1863, in Fort Mojave, Arizona, Letters Sent, in 393.

[30] Sherer, "Great Chieftains of the Mohave Indians," *Southern California Quarterly,* 48 (March, 1966), pp. 8-9. Yara tav had visited in the southern Mojave lands for years and received government food and other favors there in 1864 as is attested in various receipts dated during summer, 1864, in 734.

[31] Capt. J. Ives Fitch, commanding the fort and two companies of California Volunteers, monthly return signed May 21, 1863: Post Return.

River from the east, occurred in late March 1859, and thus should follow the episode next to be narrated. The story itself runs very closely parallel with that of W. W. Hudson, a member of Mr. Bishop's group, down to such detail as the distribution of tobacco.

The whites could not guess that they were confronting both a war and a peace faction among the Mohave. The Indians they called Pah-Utes we now know as Chemehuevis, the southernmost of Paiutes.

The narrator tells us that the Mohave had to send a scout to learn that Bishop was approaching the Colorado, the morning after his arrival at Beaver Lake. But Hudson says that the whites were guided to the river by Indians, probably Chemehuevi who were living there. The whites were told, just before starting their crossing of the Colorado, that a chief had invited them to visit his home; and it would be interesting to know which chief that was, given the very considerable differences of view that had crystallized among the Mohave as to how to treat white travelers.

When arrows began to fly at the whites while they were crossing the stream, Bishop's people took it as seriously as this Mohave narrator guessed at the time. Where Chooksa homar follows with "I think they were angry at the arrows shot at the two [white men] in the river," Bishop was saying to his people what Hudson remembered as: "We have done all we can do to convince them that we do not want to fight; and now, boys, do not fire a gun unless you think you can kill an Indian, and also scalp them if you can." As nearly as Hudson could tell, one Mohave was killed at three hundred fifty yards with a Sharp's carbine; and that must be the casualty the Mohave narrator reports.

The final encounter in this episode having occurred on March 21, Mr. Bishop remained in the neighborhood and, on April 5 by another route, with but twenty men and horses and camels but no wagons, he crossed the river and fulfilled his mission of meeting Lieutenant Beale.

The only other thing I notice here is that Bishop's party came in a very different mood and with very different intentions than did the army detachments that just preceded and followed his visit (Hoffman's reconnaissance in January, and the invasion of Mohave Valley in May). That is, it was no part of Bishop's work to involve himself in a fight with any Indians. He had a job to do that might well be thwarted by hostilities along the road. The two army expeditions came in just the other mood: their whole goal was the Mojave Valley; higher authority had already made its decision to chastise the people there insofar as might be necessary. And to engage in hostilities, while it might indicate to their superiors that they were determined officers, was not likely to detract from getting the main job done.

What we are saying, then, is that by late 1858 and early 1859 neither side, whites or Mohave, were seeing any clear indications of the differences of role or attitude among different groups on the "other" side. If any one person present was able to notice such differences, merely by looking open-eyed at the obvious conduct of people on the "other" side of the culture barrier, that person was Yara tav, as we have seen in this episode. Trying to shape the conduct of his own people so as to present something other than a threat, he failed in several attempts and finally took himself away from the immediate scene. And the war-minded people went ahead and had their small confrontation.

Episode 5. The First Soldiers Arrive

This reconnaissance occurred because highest army authority had decreed, on December 1, 1858, that a post should be placed in Mohave Valley, and on the west bank of the river, to be supplied directly overland from Southern California. So General Clarke in command of the Department of the Pacific had to try to do it that way. Major Hoffman made this flying trip, while troops were being assembled, brought down by steamer from San Francisco on their way to the Colorado River to establish the new army post. After this quick look the major reported it as impractical to try to supply an upper-Colorado post by wagon-train across the desert.

As his reports indicate, Hoffman had such a small party and found himself in such unpromising geography when he arrived near the river, that he feared ambush. Nor could he get a good view of sites from where he was. It did not seem wise to stay on the western riverbank as he had intended to do, to look for good spots for the new post. He cut the visit short and returned, after one long day's reconnaissance near the river.

Once again there are differences between the white leader's account and that of Chooksa homar; and, again, most of these variations have to do with some cultural differences and with the accident of one man being present while the other was absent. For instance, Hoffman did not arrive at night or unnoticed as Chooksa homar says; nor did the Mohave first hear of him from hunters who stumbled across his party the next morning; nor did the Mohave remain in their settlements as the soldiers moved from Beaver Lake on down to the river. These are all statements by the narrator and represent not his own observations but reports made to him by others.

Other Mohaves had seen and visited the soldiers the afternoon of their arrival, both "Pah-Utes" and Mohaves; and Hoffman had to banish Indians from his camp at sunset. He was told that chiefs would come to see him the next day. Some Indians who came that first afternoon had brought grass to sell to him for his horses.

The next morning, after a mile of trekking toward the river, he already was accompanied by groups of twenty and more Mohaves. He was questioned by both "Pah-Utes" and Mohaves, before the sharp cold of that morning was swallowed by the sun. That whites and Indians did talk, at least for a few minutes here and there, is also reported by Joseph R. Walker who was one of the guides of this expedition and who quizzed some Chemehuevi about their treatment of the Kansas City-Stockton mail parties, that had been trying to come across through Mohave Valley in recent weeks and months.

In comparing the two accounts we find that the narrator missed the late afternoon arrival of this group of whites, and also the whole next day of their short sojourn. When Chooksa homar says that many Mohave collected "in the afternoon" but stayed in their settlements, he is speaking of the day after Hoffman's arrival, a day the army men spent in working their way cautiously toward and parallel with the river, apprehensive of attack, trying to get a clear view through undergrowth. The soldiers remained fearful of attack as they cast now northward, then southward, in unfavorable terrain. The commander made up his mind that conditions did not favor this kind of work.

When the narrator continues with "Next day," and reports that Yara tav and other Mohave found the soldiers all mounted and drawn up, at that moment Hoffman and his men were on the point of departure. Hoffman felt he had seen unmistakable signs of impending attack and that the wiser course was to depart at once.

Where the two reports begin to agree closely is on the unexpectedness of the order to open fire. Hoffman ordered his men to shoot because of what we might call his view of the general attitude of the Mohave, including verbal taunts and gestures that morning, shooting of arrows into his camp the previous night, signs that there had been an attempt to bushwhack one of the sentinels, and so on. He thought that the army "face" must be maintained.

He did not realize that at the very moment before the firing, Yara tav was sending in two people to try to strike up an acquaintance. Likewise, Chooksa homar fails to mention that, while the troopers had been mounting and forming up, a Mohave was standing around exasperating the officers by yowling his imitation of the successive words of command. Hoffman says he felt he could not let such insults pass. As for the casualties from this one-sided conflict, Hoffman thought "perhaps ten or twelve" Mohave had been killed and wounded, whereas Chooksa homar knew of three wounded.

Finally, if the Mohave saw no motive in this visit by white men, neither did the major discover rhyme nor reason for the Mohaves' conduct. Each side observed that the other had appeared "ready for war," as the Mohave phrased it; or, as Hoffman had observed from the first, and as he commented concerning the Indians who dogged him out of camp on January 9, 1859, "none showed themselves who were not prepared for battle." They would all meet again soon, in Mohave Valley.

From this experience General Clarke decided not to try to bring troops and supplies the long desert route from Fort Tejon; but to base on Yuma and work most of the troops and supplies up the river on foot with support from the tiny steamers that were available. Some of these troops and impedimenta went around from the Pacific Coast, and up the Gulf of California, with transshipment from larger steamers to small, and so to Yuma; other elements of the expedition came directly across the desert to Yuma. Clarke prepared to go to Fort Yuma himself. He now felt that, quite as much as a new post in their valley, the Mohave would also need chastizing.

EPISODE 6. THE SOLDIERS ARRIVE IN FORCE

General Clarke issued his orders for the Colorado River Expedition on January 31, 1859. Hoffman was told that his force, seven companies of the 6th Infantry and an artillery detachment, would concentrate at Fort Yuma. He then was to "move up to the 35th parallel" and place a two-company post among the Mohave.

If this were accomplished without general fighting, then Hoffman was to "march against the Mohaves and Pai-Utes who lately opposed your reconnaissance," and who must be "brought to submission." The outcome must be agreement by the Indians of "no opposition to establishment of posts or roads in and through their country"; and security for the "property and lives of whites traveling through their country." In letters later that year, after the post had been established, Clarke's intentions were stated further: "the security to the route on which you are posted"—the 35the parallel overland wagon route scouted out by Lieutenant Beale—"is the object to be kept in view"; and "the Post was placed on the River to give protection to Emigrants and the mail and full security both must have."[32] In a larger sense Clarke also felt that the huge expense of sending the expedition and maintaining a garrison were necessary to ensure the whites' future safety in the whole region. If the Mohave were not subdued, "their impunity might influence those below to render the lower route [the Gila Trail] equally perilous."[33]

If no fighting proved to be necessary, Clarke specified that the major must take hostages: those chiefs who had attacked Hoffman's reconnaissance party, and others as "hostages for their future conduct." Such captives must be given up to him, otherwise Hoffman was to lay waste the Mohaves' crops and to promise them he would not allow them "hereafter to cultivate their lands in peace." After all this had been accomplished, Hoffman was to leave the garrison in its new post and bring the larger number of troops back down to Fort Yuma.

This was a large order. It meant moving and supplying hundreds of soldiers through very difficult marching country in the oppressive climate of the Colorado River bottoms with summer coming on. Very few supplies for man or beast would be found en route, and the weakly powered little steamers that would carry food and equipment had not been working the river long enough for reliable knowledge of the danger spots and the shifting sands in the stream. On the other hand the men themselves were not recruits, and they were fit for this trip. This was the famous 6th Infantry which had long been on the frontiers and had just finished a 2,100-mile walk in going from one duty station to another.[34] As it proved, the expedition lost many mules and cattle but no soldiers on its way upriver.

As for the great council Hoffman convened soon after his arrival in the valley, we have found no white man's record of the conversations between army commander and Mohave chieftains. This is a real pity because, if Private Bandel is correct, the statements had to be relayed back and forth from English into Spanish, and Mohave, through two interpreters. This reminds us that the record does not indicate that even one of the northern Mohave could as yet speak English—although in 1858 Lieutenant Ives found one man who had memorized several dozen words and drove the explorer wild by repeating these words in various combinations. It looks as if Yara tav was, still in 1863, unable to speak in the white man's language. So, the question whether Hoffman did get across to the Mohave the message he passed to the interpreters must remain unanswered at this time, as also the question whether Hoffman realized just how intransigent was the chief Mohave spokesman, Homose-quahote, all during this meeting.

<hr/>

[32] January 31 orders in *Report, War, 1859,* pp. 407-408; the later quotations from Clarke to Major Lewis A. Armistead, May 29, 1859, and August 3, 1859: Records of the War Department, Fort Mojave. Letters Received, 1859-1890, USNA.

[33] To the Adjutant General, Los Angeles, March 21, 1859, *Report, War, 1859,* pp. 403-404.

[34] "Yesar" in *Weekly Alta California,* May 7, 1859.

As for choosing the hostages, that was done by the Mohave, and here is what A. L. Kroeber had to say about that part of the episode.

The war-loving chief Asikahôta comes off very well. He is still ready to die, but he is not going to be taken; and he is not. Aratêve stands at the side and for once is not quoted as speaking; it is his relatives and associates who volunteer to become hostages, out of a sort of *noblesse oblige*. Among them are the Americans' old friend, and partner of Aratêve, Cairook (here called Avi-havasuch) and his kin.

If hostages were to be given, it was a mistake to let the hostile chiefs defiantly refuse to go, but to allow the kinsmen of the pro-American leaders to make up the number. Hoffman in his report boasts of the number of chiefs, chiefs' sons, and nephews got among the hostages, evidently wholly ignoring their established inclinations and records as individuals—all Indians were just Indians, unless they were chiefs. Hoffman had a strong enough force that he might perhaps have accomplished something constructive. Perhaps not; perhaps there had to be blood-letting before a proud and successful people would bow to superior strength. But he displayed his strength to compel a cowed submission, and then promptly marched out of the country carrying away friendlies as captives, and leaving it to Major Armistead—with a force one quarter the size of his—to pick up the pieces in combat when Hoffman's hollow settlement finally cracked, four months later.

Hoffman had faced six chiefs, three of them hostile to the whites and three (Avi-havasuts, Qolho qorau, and Yara tav) potentially friendly. He had asked for ten hostages: the six chiefs of bands in Mohave Valley; the one chief who had menaced his reconnaissance party in January; and any three Mohave who had attacked the Rose-Hedgpeth emigrant train in 1858. He now had nine hostages assembled anyhow, who had no idea how long they would be held or with what result.

In a sense this episode shows two resolute men in bloodless conflict, and we know too little of how each of them, Hoffman and Homose-quahote, would have explained his actions at that time. Certainly Hoffman had not availed himself of information ready at hand as to the personal attitudes of individual Mohave leaders. On the way upriver he had met one of those Mohaves who was disposed to be friendly with the whites, the chief Ho-mar-rah-tav who lived far to the south of Mohave Valley. Hoffman knew that this chief had been given "papers" by recent explorers including Amiel Whipple and Joseph C. Ives; and Hoffman had a positive recommendation of Ho-mar-rah-tav from his own trusted subordinate, Captain Burton.[35] But the major seems not to have thought of conversing with this well-informed and well-disposed Mohave.

Probably Hoffman was intent on carrying out the orders he had received and winding up the expedition quickly. He was a most successful career officer in the post-Mexican War army; he knew that General Clarke's good repute as well as his own future career hung in the balance here, with the Secretary of War and the General-in-Chief, Winfield Scott, watching this affair very closely. I am assuming that everything in the situation inclined Hoffman to act with despatch,

---

[35] Hoffman met "the chief of those who live in the lower end of the valley," Needles Valley, at the improvised Fort Gaston which had been established about 65 miles north of Yuma on the river to service this expedition: Hoffman to Clarke's adjutant, Camp at Bill Williams Fork, April 11, 1859: Records of the War Department, Letters Received, 1822-1860, AGO. He merely commented, "I shall see him again." On Ho-mar-rah-tav, see Peter R. Brady's report of Oct. 9, 1860, and quotation from Major Haller's letter of Jan. 28, 1862, in Sherer, "Great Chieftains," p. 5. He was receiving government food on the reservation in 1865-1867, as Ho marrt tow or Homororow, where he was considered one of the "captains."

concluding quickly and avoiding any aspects that might delay matters or trail off into subtleties. He put together a group of hostages, moved most of his troops out of this formidable desert, and pushed back down to Yuma where General Clarke was waiting.

To put it more charitably, since all this had come his way some four months earlier, Hoffman had been exceedingly busy, beginning with the move of troops out of Benicia Barracks and continuing on through all the cross-country and steamer-to-steamerlet operations required to deliver seven companies of foot soldiers to the upper Colorado. All this work militated against any side trip to Los Angeles to talk to people who might have something to tell him about the Mohave. Another man might have found a way to inform himself: after all, Hoffman had spent days with old Joe Walker on the reconnaissance trip, and he brought with him in the Colorado River Expedition the head chief of the Quechans, Pascual, who in half a day's talk could have given Hoffman all that he would need to know of the undercurrents of personalism in Mohave public affairs.

As for Homose-quahote, again I quote A. L. Kroeber's estimation:

Hoffman lets the avowedly hostile Asikahôta go, and jails volunteers from the peace party instead: And one can see why. Had he given orders to lay hands on him, Asikahôta would have resisted and struck, would have been shot, the rest of the Mohave would inevitably have been involved, with many of them massacred and perhaps some losses among the troops, and the part of the tribe not present at the meeting would have been outraged and turned completely hostile. The officer's decision was prudent, at least for the moment; but at the expense of Asikahôta's having won a kind of moral victory through his singlemindedness and stubborn courage.

The other side of the picture is that Asikahôta's attitude completely lacked any sense of responsibility toward his community. They might be slaughtered and lose their lands and liberty as a result of his intransigence: that affected him as little as the prospect of his own death. The one thing he holds to unswervingly is his ego inflation attained through being ready to die by violence. A wilfully limited personality, successful thereby in instilling social respect, yet capable only of social destructiveness in its potential effects.

Still another angle is that after all his talk of liking to die, he was still alive after inciting several unsuccessful attacks. It would appear that the Mohave were more realistic than intransigent in their expectation of conduct on the battlefield. A kwanami seemingly kept his reputation if he showed bravery; he did not have to die to vindicate his courage if the fight went against his side. Again, ego exaltation looms bigger than tribal considerations, but these give him an out: if the rest run away, he too may run, provided he has shown bravery in the incitement and attack.

These professional diers must have been a tense, self-centered, somewhat pathological type among the river Yumans, at once created and supported by a halo of highest social esteem evolved by the culture to accord to them. It seems significant that they were diers and not killers, from the viewpoint of their society: we have no record that they ever killed or even overtly bullied members of their own tribe. There is clearly a large masochistic component in their character.

Turning to Cairook's actions and attitude, where he says to Asikahôta, 'Well, if you're afraid [to go as a hostage], I'll go'; here he clinches his case by saying in effect 'I will do what you fear to do.' Again the ultimate appeal is to courage. The policies are opposite, the values the same. Cairook was volunteering to undergo imprisonment, perhaps hanging, as we see in the very last sentences of this episode. A masochistic ingredient is again evident. The original motivation may have been reasoned prudence in the face of perceived American superiority, as it was vainglory on the opposite side; but in crisis the moral values were the same. How often may similar motivations have been at work elsewhere, in the split between 'progressives' and 'conservatives,' 'friendlies' and 'hostiles,' without the unknowingly insolent white Americans being aware of the fact—among Hopi, Dakota, or Iroquois?

EPISODE 7. PEACEFUL RELATIONS WITH THE MILITARY

The calm and workaday feeling of this episode is reflected in the main source we have found among the whites,[36] for this same brief interval between the departure of Hoffman with most of the soldiers, at the end of April, and the increasingly tense days in June and July, after the breakout of the hostages from Fort Yuma that will be discussed in the next episode.

During this quiet time both Armistead and the Mohave were thinking of the Walapai. As Armistead put it, "The Mohaves have on one or two occasions said, that the Whalupi wanted to make peace; my reply was for them to come in—I expect to see them some time this month." The department commander at San Francisco was worried about Paiute hostility, and Armistead, having had his own report of hostilities in that direction, went out twenty-five miles to the westward to look. But he found nothing and suspected that worries to the west were groundless.

He, like other whites who were in touch with the Mohave during those early months of occupation, found them "the best behaved Indians I have ever seen. They are the only Indians I have ever seen, that I think *might* be civilized." As for those who lived beyond the view of the garrison—Walapai to the east, Paiute to the south, north, and west—Armistead suffered from limitations that afflicted all the later commandants of that isolated outpost: no transport to speak of, too few soldiers for him to plan anything comprehensive in traveling about or coming to know the neighboring peoples, and a rock-bottom situation for food, clothing, and supplies. His view in those early months was much the same as that of some later commandants, if for a different reason: "My opinion as to the treatment of the Whalupi and Payutes is to shoot them whenever you can, as I believe it impossible to keep them from stealing horses, mules, or anything else, when a good opportunity offers. These Indians, the Payutes especially, are generally in a half starved state—they steal to eat—sometimes, to live—They will always be troublesome and difficult to manage, not from their numbers, but from the character of the country which they inhabit . . . . " Here was an early prediction of what gradually became the Paiute War, just a few years later.

EPISODE 8. THE CAPTIVE MOHAVE ESCAPE

At least in hindsight this incident was expectable enough. The hostages were never, so far as we know, given any idea how long they might have to remain in jail, far from home. The newspaper correspondent "Yesar" found them languishing after several weeks of confinement. And, of course, these prisoners were not just any nine Mohave. Several of them had well-established habits of leadership and decision. Prodded by one, after a time all decided to act.

After the breakout the whites thought, as usual, that they had killed many more than they really did. It was general report that most of the hostages were

---

[36] Armistead's letter of June 14, 1859.

now dead. What is more surprising to me is that so little memory of this incident survived among white men, at least to judge from the absence of conventional references in old newspapers, histories, and official documents. The young chief Qolho qorau, then about twenty-five years old, survived the century and played a major role on the River Reservation, becoming the leading chief there in 1874; but I have never seen this escape of his mentioned by any white man, after Peter Brady in 1860.

As for reverberations of this incident, General Clarke at San Francisco heard of it even before Major Armistead could report the facts to him. He ordered Armistead to "Take a firm stand with the Mohaves and demand their surrender and inform them that the demand will be enforced."[37] In view of later events this may have been wise counsel; but Armistead saw no cause for alarm and did not attempt any punitive measures. The Secretary of War concluded that "The escape of the hostages was to be expected if an opportunity offered. Of itself, it will not be made the ground of hostilities against the Mohaves." And, "The plan of taking Indian hostages for indefinite periods, is attended with no useful results, but rather the contrary, and will be prohibited.[38]

The question remains whether the taking of hostages, and the emotional impact of the return of all of them but two, had its part in bringing on the final crisis in Mohave Valley.

EPISODE 9. OPEN WAR WITH THE AMERICAN TROOPS

The brief reports of Major Armistead of this crisis between the army and the Mohave closely resemble Chooksa homar's account. As should be expected, the passage of time is not rendered exactly as white men are wont to do. Thus, the killing of the herdsman occurred about July 20, whereas to work forward in the Mohave narrative, leaving reasonable numbers of days at each stage, would put this event in late June as Chooksa homar reckoned it, rather than in late July when it did occur. So also with the narrator's remembrance of longer intervals of time, those coming in between the major episodes of which this reminiscence is composed. He recalled the intervals themselves, but did not remember them in the same way a white man would have done at the time. He did not make the intervals long enough. I suspect that Chooksa homar was using some conventional phrases for these time lapses, unique to his own viewpoint or to Mohave culture. We cannot now tell when we are seeing one of these conventions, which could include such phrases as "a year later" or, as in this episode, "five days after." Allowing for the fading of events in memory after forty-four years had passed, it still looks as if the passing of time between memorable events did not have much importance for Chooksa homar.

Three other things seem worth emphasizing as they become obvious in this episode. First, the time was past if it had ever been, when all Mohave would feel obligated to take some part in every incident of war. Although the narrator twice

[37] Clarke to Armistead, June 30, 1859, Fort Mojave, Letters Received, 1859-1890, in 393.

[38] Endorsement by the Acting Secretary on Armistead's letter to Department headquarters, July 3, 1859: in Letters Received, 1822-1860, AGO; and printed in *Report, War, 1859*, pp. 415-416, in the form of notification to the General-in-Chief, Winfield Scott.

says that "all" the Mohave gathered together for this final attack on the whites, at the end of the episode we recall that there were Mohave living far to the south who had taken no part in this final battle. This accords with Peter Brady's statement in 1860, that from Ho-mar-rah-tav and his people only a few had come north for the fighting. He and the rest of his part of the tribe stayed far south of Mohave Valley, and they had no part in any hostilities against the whites. I wonder whether some of the smaller and shifting settlements in the south, some perhaps not more than one- or two-days' travel north of Yuma, even heard of the events of this episode until all were concluded.

In brief, this new situation with the United States Army detachment embedded in Mohave Valley was already worlds apart from the older usages of war, whereby a party would be gathered together for the long overland trip to strike the Pima and Maricopa. The southern Mohave must have taken part in those raids, especially since some of those attacks originated with invitation from the Yuma as had happened in 1857. But this new situation of white penetration of their country had the curious effect of leaving the southern Mohave isolated from the war.

Second, the narrator seems very clear on the point that this was the time of permanent division between two groups of Mohave, one group inclining toward the white Americans and toward peace, the other leaning toward traditional viewpoints, toward the ancestral home in Mohave Valley, and toward a more narrowly tribal orientation for the future. One was the party of Yara tav, of the late chief Cairook, of Qolho qorau, and Ho-mar-rah-tav in the south; the other was led by the tribal head chief, Homose-quahote, with the support of other chiefs and kwanami in Mohave Valley, including Asukit, now a kwanami and soon to become a band chief. The peace party moving south out of the valley into lands that would in time become the Colorado River Reservation, comprised substantial parts of four clans: Neolge (the clan of Yara tav, Chooksa homar, and Asukit), Mus, Oach, and Malika.[39]

However, that this was but a temporary move we may assume from later episodes of this narrative. There seems to be no specific record that indicates just when Yara tav made the final shift of home and fortune, or how many people went with him, or whether any white people were instrumental in influencing the move at that time.

Episode 10. Peace and Return

There is much in this brief episode that is important for the history of the Mohave, and for understanding the long and complex history of accommodation between white man and Mohave. But I have not seen documents authored by whites that would give us any further explanations. How many Mohave had been resident south of the valley before 1859, how many now joined them there—there are no sure answers. Seemingly the southern Mohave still took little or no part in any of the events in the valley. The narrator's statement that "those who had settled there before, stayed," I assume to mean that Ho-mar-rah-tav's

---

[39] Information from Dan Welsh to A. L. Kroeber, in 1953.

southerners did not trek to Fort Mojave to meet with Major Armistead. Like all Mohave at all times, they would come later in the ordinary round of visiting.

Likewise, we do not know how many of those who had temporarily gone southward, and now returned to meet with the soldiers, remained in Mohave Valley. One way to get at this would have been through the names of those who were put forward when Armistead asked how many were captains. To some degree those captains who in 1864 or 1865 moved to the River Reservation can be found named in records there; but we have no names for 1859, either from Chooksa homar or from whites' sources I have seen for 1859.

And we are left with questions about what the term "captain" signified both to the whites and the Mohaves. My assumption has been that one who was here made "captain" by the army had most likely been what Chooksa homar calls a "head man," or an "old man," in his narrative. Some of these "captains" must have been chiefs before the Anglo-American conquest. The record for the Colorado River Reservation is clearer, and there we find people who had ranked as chiefs before 1859 (Ho-mar-rah-tav) or very soon thereafter (Qolho qorau) dubbed as "captains" after Yara tav took up residence there and was considered to be the principal chief. What I conclude from all this is that the conquest brought very little dislocation in the normal, and to us unknown, processes by which men moved toward and held prestigious rank among the Mohave. This would be particularly true, of course, for shamans, whom I have not seen mentioned in records left by army officers or Indian agents from 1859 through 1873, but who are discussed by some of those responding to the army's questionnaire sent to officers throughout the Department of Arizona in mid-1874.[40]

So, although Chooksa homar's narrative and the parallel sources of white authorship do not provide a panoramic view of all the leadership roles among the Mohave in 1859, it looks as if Major Armistead appointed "captains" in Mohave Valley just as Major Heintzelman had done among the Quechan six or seven years before. What is not clear is whether the army officers rejected anyone who was recommended, whether some here appointed "captains" had simply been kwanami before, or whether any other multiple roles were created in this act of 1859, such as shaman-captain or chief-captain.

The third thing we notice here is the beginning of a return to a different kind of narrative, which we have seen before in the episodes relating to the Cocopa and the Maricopa peace mission, and which characterize the later episodes bearing on the Walapai and Yavapai, the Chemehuevi, and the Calloway murder. We are virtually certain that Chooksa homar himself participated in few of the events contained in all those episodes, just as he is unlikely to have witnessed everything he tells us here in connection with Asikahôta's final submission to Major Armistead. In between, in the episodes dealing with the emigrant train, Bishop's and Hoffman's visits, and the Colorado River Expedition, Chooksa homar was frequently discussing things he had himself

---

[40] See U.S. Army, Department of Arizona, Report on Arizona Indians, 1874: 63 folders, ms. P-D 3, in Bancroft Library, University of California, Berkeley, and discussion and summary of one of the responses, by Arthur Woodward, "John G. Bourke on the Arizona Apache, 1874," *Plateau*, 16 (Oct. 1943), 33-44.

witnessed. It was notable that in those episodes he left out sections of the action that he had not seen. From here on, then, we suspect that he tells piece by piece in no given order what he learned from others except where he says that he saw it, or was there.

One cannot tell simply by reading this episode whether the Mohave were quite as ready to combine with whites against the Walapai as the narrator may be suggesting. While the Mojave and Walapai have sometimes been put down as traditionally hostile to one another, almost all the information for this conclusion comes to us, perforce, from post-1864 conditions and witnesses. The most western of Walapai used to spend time in the Colorado River lowlands, perhaps during a part of every year. The Mohave knew them personally. There must have been some intermarriage. In one known instance of travel through Walapai country, Yara tav showed uneasiness only when reaching the farther, eastern edge of Walapai territory, but was willing enough to go and return through this neighboring territory, although suspicious and watchful while he did it. What I am assuming is that it would be no easy task to turn the Mohave into war against these nearest neighbors, who had never been enemies before, so far as I know.

That the army wanted help against the Walapai whenever it might be needed, I have no doubt. The words put in Major Armistead's mouth I would credit, when Chooksa homar has him say: "Some of the Walapai are bad and fighting me. Don't help them! If they become worse, you and we will go to fight them." Simple practices of divide and conquer were familiar to the frontier army, and higher authority time and again urged such a policy. Frontier commanders with their tiny garrisons, and in a frightening isolation from supply or support, no doubt reinvented this policy over and over again. In the next episode we will see how, finally and with much difficulty, tribe was indeed set against tribe in western Arizona.

All these and other aspects of making a recognizable political framework that the whites could understand, drawing "friendlies" closer so as the better to deal with the "hostiles," all were still in very early stages. Before the Colorado River tribes could be further organized by the whites, the Civil War intervened and for two years such matters as we have been discussing were more or less in suspension.

As for the recognition of "about ten men" as chiefs or captains, this involves one further aspect of the culture that may long since have faded beyond our power to reconstruct or recall it. Specifically, did clan members identify certain locations in Mohave Valley as theirs, for purposes of residence and farming, as well as for nationalistic historical identification with their own past? Another question is whether, if there were such clan foci still in 1859, members of the various clans were still to be found living in or near these focal points.

A. L. Kroeber had this to say on the matter: "Settlements normally consisted of kinsmen in the male line, and thereby of men in the same clan, but there was said to be usually several places thus 'belonging' to each clan, especially if it was large."[41] And Gwegwi nuor, who had been a young man in 1859, when listing the clans called them the "individual land owners;" then, after naming them, added

----

[41] *A Mohave Historical Epic,* University of California Anthropological Records, 11 (Berkeley, 1951), p. 71.

that "The present generation [as of 1935] still have their names but would not locate the properties I am sure."[42] A reading of the historical epic narrated by Inyo-kutavêre shows the section of this literary-historical narrative explaining the Mohave quasi-historical memory of this whole matter. In the published *Epic*, A. L. Kroeber entitled that section "The Taking of the Land by Totemic Kin Groups."[43]

But as Kroeber discovered when in 1903 and thereafter he tried to reconstruct the picture of land occupation as it had been, the very last men to whom this had any meaning were even then passing away.

The detail was growing faint in their minds; but, more significant was the fact that this information was not being passed on to younger people for their telling, largely because this landholding pattern could not be made into narratives vivid enough to hold people's attention through the long evenings of declamation. So, with the tribal memory as also with the written and oral records of the whites, most "history" is lost when it fails to enter the living memory of the very next generation. And once forgotten, most of it will not be found again. In this instance, what was lost by 1900 or 1910 was the historical-territorial pattern that might enable us to know any relationships between clan, territory, and chieftainship.

Kroeber also found it impossible to piece out the picture of aboriginal landholdings by joining together information from several different oral accounts. As he put it, "I came to realize that no Mohave could 'continue' the narration of another. The versions differ too much through being after all individually refantasied, as I would construe the core to be of what the Mohave mean by 'dreaming.' "[44]

EPISODE 11. WAR WITH YAVAPAI AND WALAPAI

Here are ten discrete incidents, held together by the presence in them of Walapai or Yavapai or both, and all drawn from that period of outright hostilities which resulted from white men's earliest mining and settlement in what is today northwest and north-central Arizona. Oddly enough, in giving us just these ten incidents, and by discussing them in isolation from their contexts, what the narrator has done is to offer us something which reads not unlike the reports white men made at the time. The main difference is that Chooksa homar does not do any moralizing beyond what he felt the white man would expect to hear.

What I am saying is that it is difficult enough to learn much simply by reading anybody's barebones narrative that does not begin with the first contacts between Indian and white and continue on from there, keeping in view the cumulative effects of those contacts and of the changes these produced in behavior as time went by. It may not matter so much where we declare the "beginning" of white-Indian contacts to be: whether with earliest Spanish

---

[42] Quoted in Lorraine Sherer, *The Clan System of the Fort Mojave Indians* (Los Angeles, 1965), p. 25, from his memoirs dictated in 1935 and a manuscript in the Fort Mojave Tribe records.

[43] *A Mohave Historical Epic*, pp. 103 ff.

[44] Ibid., p. 71.

exploration; or with the coming of the French-American, Mexican-American, and Anglo-American trappers; or, for that matter, whether we begin as I will very briefly do below, with some of the first Anglo-Americans to mine and to settle in northern Arizona. In any case, incidents taken from 1866 to 1873, as Chooksa homar has done in this chapter, cannot really be made intelligible without some historical background to illuminate the specific events.

It may be pertinent to remind ourselves first of all that very few white observers and participants in the first wave of settlers, from the 1850s through the early 1870s, thought of "Indian war" in northern Arizona in any but a certain very limited way. They very rarely if ever thought of themselves as making war on the Indians and on the native way of life—a war that started when the first sizeable groups of would-be miners and ranchers entered the region in 1862 and 1863. That their very presence, and the manner in which they gripped the land and water and rebuffed the people, could constitute "war," very few of them would have accepted as a reasonable view.

Neither, then, did they think of the Indian as carrying on a more or less steady resistance to white man's war, a sort of slow-burning guerrilla operation. At first this native effort aimed at mere survival, and sooner or later, as the country filled up slowly with whites and the Indians' scope of movement and food and water resources were steeply reduced, began to look to the whites like an exceedingly perverse attempt to kill all white men. During those first years, up to some time in 1865 in both Walapai and Yavapai country, if the Indian stayed out of sight for a few months most of the whites assumed that there was peace, since there was no obvious war.

So, most of the time in much of the Walapai and Yavapai country, the white man identified war only if all the surrounding country was full of hostilities by Indians. Or he called it "war" when his own, the army troops, were conducting some rather large campaign. Other hostilities were usually written off to the bad character of the Indians, their refusal or lack of capacity to become civilized, or, simply, to their unwillingness to abide conditions of peace and quiet.

A few white people knew differently. Some of them were already there by 1860 or came soon thereafter; and they knew from personal experience that hostilities had begun at the very beginning of white occupation of northern Arizona and had continued ever since. Daniel Conner's memoirs are graphic in this sense, as he describes the Walker Party's first encounter with Yavapai, showing how relationships were broken within the very first few days and were never thereafter reestablished at all. Charlie Genung, who also came in '63, points out that by the end of that year it wasn't really safe to travel from Tucson up to the area that later became Prescott, with fewer than five men in a group. He had done it himself but he knew the risk he was running.[45] King Woolsey, one of the early settlers living just at the southeastern edge of Yavapai country—and a bitter and determined Indian killer—put it accurately when he wrote that "the war commenced with the Yavapais in the winter of 1863, and has continued ever since."[46]

---

[45] Genung, "My First Year in Arizona," Southwest Museum transcript of ms. in Sharlot Hall Museum, Prescott, Arizona.

[46] Quoted in *Weekly Arizona Miner,* June 2, 1870. Of course he meant that the Yavapai had started the war.

What this amounts to is that those whites who did not face the fact of war tended constantly to expect the coming of war. They feared Indian plots, seeing a specter of mass uprising in even the smallest and most local events. A great deal of paper was sent from place to place reporting rumors of impending transtribal attacks on all the whites in Arizona. The fact that at rare intervals such a thing might indeed have been attempted elsewhere[47] was remembered by some of the white people. I have seen nothing to indicate that these whites knew of the much earlier messianic uprisings that had studded the history of north-central Mexico. The very situation in which the whites found themselves suggested all these fears. If we wonder today at army officers who would connive at Indians' murder of Indians, or if we stand aghast at local newspapers that would exult when another Indian was shot to death and thereby "put on the reservation," as William H. Hardy liked to phrase it, we should remember that these whites were prey to fears and to economic pressures that overtested their personal stability on many occasions.

They feared, at least until 1867 or 1868, that the army presence in Arizona was proving too expensive, and showing too few results, to be politically or even technically feasible to continue. When the Colorado River Expedition was well in hand, General Clarke estimated that supplies for the new post would have to come from the Pacific Coast, many of them by steamer through the Gulf of California, at an expense around $300 the ton. For many years, hay for the army's horses had to be imported into Arizona at staggering cost. And one could shovel any number of small infantry posts into the Arizona landscape without making any discernible gain in pacification of Indians. The posts were too small and their patrols moved too slowly to make any real dent. We should remember not that there was a Fort Mohave here and a Fort McDowell there, with a fine mythic impression of serried ranks of dragoons sweeping through the staggering hordes of Indians. Let us instead remember that an army post, and an Indian band nearby, tended to even out at about the same number of armed people each. Often this number hovered between twenty and forty.

After the Colorado River Expedition departed Mohave Valley, and after Armistead made peace with the Mohave, the number of soldiers at that fort fell first from hundreds to one hundred sixty-five, and then to about forty, and that is where it stayed and the number to which it returned when the fort was reoccupied in May 1863. When in mid-June of 1867 a new commandant came to that post with a mandate to make an aggressive, punitive war on the Walapai in their home villages, this Lieutenant Colonel William R. Price found somewhat fewer than thirty-seven soldiers ready for what a self-respecting cavalryman could call duty. It was September of the year before he had as many soldiers as Armistead had commanded during mid-1859.

So, we should think of these years from 1862 to 1873 as a period of extreme fear, privation, and uncertainty for most of the whites who spent any time there. My impression is that almost as many whites left that northern section of the territory during those years as entered it. Many of the first settlements were

[47] Forbes, *Warriors of the Colorado,* pp. 326-330, for an account of Antonio Garra's uprising of 1851 in Southern California; and George W. and Helen P. Beattie, *Heritage of the Valley* . . . (Pasadena, 1939), pp. 234-235, on the Juan Antonio tumult in 1855.

abandoned for lack of any economic basis. All this made for a bitterness in white-Indian relations that has not been fully understood. And if we were to say that central and northern Arizona was a no-man's land for whites during those years, the same was true for the Indians still trying to live there.

They were sooner driven to desperation than any but a very few whites realized at the time. To cut them off from one spring was to force some serious change in the native round of life. To reduce the supply of game was to threaten the Indian with famine, especially if some other source of food had failed at that same time. If the whites were fighting the Indians at the season of planting, the result was "great suffering . . . for months our camp was filled with men, women and children, begging for something to eat," as Major Heintzelman reported from Yuma in 1853.

In the upper country where the natives farmed less or not at all, and depended heavily upon gathering and hunting, events could snowball disastrously against chances for survival. Some Yavapai had the habit of a little farming and gathering of mesquite beans in the Colorado River lowlands, also traveling far inland nearer their homes for hunting, and to find saguaro, mescal, and many other plants. But if the Colorado did not overflow its banks—if both farming and mesquite failed—and if the white man was barring them from hunting in the hills—then these Yavapai could starve, very quickly.

During the first year of occupation of the Yavapai homeland by whites, Pauline Weaver stated what would be the Yavapai and Walapai predicament, beginning for some of them in the winter of 1863. A Yavapai captain had pointed out to Weaver that "the Indians on the river would not allow his people to geather seeds there and if the whites here [Walnut Grove] did not allow him to geather it here he would have to join the hostile Indians in order to live . . . ." And Weaver added that "It is hard to ceep a hunkry Indian from stealing and almost as hard to keep the whites from making an indiscriminade Sioughter of them for Stealing . . . I would like to know if enything can be done for those Oborigines that are inclined to be peasable."[48]

During the time of the incidents discussed here by Chooksa homar, the Indians of northern Arizona were coming to a desperate enough pass that tribal amities of long standing were beginning to break down. It was not as so many whites imagined, that Apache, Pima, and Yuma would somehow make friends for the first time and all descend on the white man all together. It was now a question whether tribes that had once associated in a prevailingly peaceable way could go on like that, or whether Walapai and Mohave, Chemehuevi and Mohave, or some Yavapai and the Mohave, would turn on each other or even be turned against each other by the white man.

These ten episodes, beginning with one in 1866 and ending with another in 1872-1873, are selected from the period when the old associations of peace were indeed breaking down, and when old enmities were sharpening under the pressure exerted by the whites. At the time the first of these ten incidents began, there had been war in Yavapai country for three years, and Indian resistance in Walapai country was also becoming more emphatic, probably for the first time. Whites then and now think of the "war" in Walapai country as commencing in

---

[48] Weaver to Charles Poston, Walnut Grove, Oct. 30, 1864, in 234.

1865. This is probably accurate enough in that the Walapai seem to have been scandalized, and much more inclined to turn on the whites, after the murder of two of their chiefs—one in April 1865 in the south, and the other in the north on April 8, 1866.[49] Since Chooksa homar's narrative does not enter into the intricacies of the ensuing guerrilla war in Walapai country we will not follow it here; but that was such a complex struggle that in trying to recall it Chooksa homar might well have inverted the order of some events and misdated others.

That unheralded conflict among settlers, miners, freighters, soldiers, and townsmen on one side, and among harried and autonomous bands of Walapai and Yavapai on the other, was in fact not an organized war at all. It was simply so much deadly conflict among small anarchic groups, of which only the United States Army units acknowledged any higher leadership or central organization. It would be almost as difficult to trace the events in one delimited zone, or to follow the fortunes of any small group, as it would now be to try to reconstruct the day-to-day guerrilla warfare of Filipinos and United States detachments after the Spanish-American War. Something has been done in recent years to disentangle the events of the Walapai War with the whites.[50]

All this may help us to recognize that the ten episodes in this chapter of Chooksa homar's narrative are but a handful of the many ambushes and raids, from a very extensive pattern of hostilities of all kinds. Perhaps we can best summarize this view by quoting from a well-known report of Indian Agent John C. Dunn, written at the territorial capital, Prescott, on May 23, 1865: "The condition of affairs stated as probable to ensue in my letter now exists. We have a war waged upon us by the Yavapais, Hualapis & Apache Mohaves, which has been brought on by the wanton and cruel aggressions of not only the settlers but by the troops placed here for protection & peace."[51]

Now, for specific comment on the various incidents contained within this chapter. One might begin by asking hôw the narrator could possibly know the details of the killing of George Leihy and his clerk in 1866? I assume that the answer is the obvious one, that the Mohave were still then friendly with several different bands of Western Yavapai. Yara tav in particular had close touch with one band that came to the Colorado River Reservation whenever hunger drove

---

[49] John C. Dunn, Prescott, May 23, 1865, in *Walapai Papers,* cit. supra; and Capt. E. C. Ledyard to Gen. J. M. Mason, April 10 and 18, 1866, and Capt. Dan Loosley, Fort Mohave, April 12, 1866, in 734. The earlier was "Anasa"; the latter, Wauba or Wassa Yuma. His murder has been so often misdated as to year, ascribed to other tribes, and described out of context, that it is worth emphasizing that Ledyard heard the story two days afterward on the spot, from the white murderers. He quietly listened to the killer's "cover" story, then let his bugler chat with the men who told him the real story.

[50] In the process the people doing the work had to restudy and elaborate the whole previous picture of Walapai living zones and organization. See Robert C. Euler, "Walapai Culture History" (Ph.D., University of New Mexico, 1958), and the several exhaustive monographs by Henry L. Dobyns which I have seen together in one place only in Docket 90 (The Hualapai Indians of the Hualapai Reservation, Arizona, Petitioners, vs. The United States of America, Defendant) in the Indian Claims Commission files, Washington, D.C. In due time, when the Hualapai claim is in all respects a finished item, this docket will pass into the National Archives to remain with others of the Indians' claims cases carried through since the 1940s. As but one brief indication of the shift in understanding on account of this work, Dobyns presents the Walapai as having comprised twelve bands, not the seven groupings shown in the cooperative volume *Walapai Ethnography* (Menasha, Wis., 1935). See also Dobyns and Euler, *Wauba Yuma's People* . . . (Prescott, Ariz., 1970), for still further understandings.

[51] In 234.

them to it. But if the Mohave could easily know the story, why did they not tell the whites who were upset for years afterward by this event, and who were always trying to find out who the murderers had been? At least part of the answer may be that the guerrilla war in northern Arizona was not so far advanced, nor people's feelings yet so nervous or bitter, that Yara tav was yet being forced to act as a spy or a turncoat. I can guess that the Mohave "kept still" about the Leihy affair partly because they saw what a terrible amount of feeling it had raised among the whites. As occurred both earlier and later than this, the blame would be put on some other tribe, someone to whom one owed no debts of friendship, in this case the Tonto Apache whom the whites might suspect anyway.

Why the Yavapai killed these three people is impossible to know without some further direct report. Possibly Leihy was killed by an ill mixture of unrequited hunger and hot bullets, as follows. In mid-1866 increasing hostilities had brought on both a crisis of feeling among the whites,[52] and a vigorous resistance among Indians who were facing starvation. To quote Ralph Ogle: "Traffic almost stopped west of Prescott; [wagon] trains moved with military escorts. Lieutenant Oscar Hutton [of the so-called Arizona Volunteers, a Territorial armed force] sent to the region in July, killed no Indians at first; but he destroyed their resources and thus made the situation worse by leaving the bands more destitute than before. On August 11 his command and a train he was escorting through Skull Valley were attacked [as likely, simply confronted] by one hundred and fifty impoverished warriors who demanded the contents of the wagons. A parley followed, but it broke up in a severe battle in which the Indians were worsted with heavy loss. Leihy . . . considered the victory a defeat."[53]

Superintendent Leihy was indeed very close by when all this happened, and he inquired at the scene just afterward. It looks very much as if the surviving Yavapai in this group thought of him from then on as in league with the Arizona Volunteers.

To show that Chooksa homar was merely relating a story he had heard, whether at second or third-hand we do not know, the whites' account indicates that there were not one but two Indians with Leihy. One was a Maricopa acting as interpreter, the other a Yavapai being brought back to the Colorado River Reservation as a prisoner, to be turned over to his own chief.

As for the next episode, a Chemehuevi trying to cash a check, the arrival of soldiers at La Paz, and conferences with Yara tav, I cannot identify such a sequence of events. My guess is that Chooksa homar transposed and recombined some happenings here, recalling a well-known case in 1871 when Mohaves were discovered changing large bills at the La Paz post office—money presumably taken by Yavapai in the ambush of a stagecoach near Wickenburg (not too far from the scene of Leihy's wagon ambush in 1866). I feel that these events are placed too early in time, too, because they indicate the whites pressing in on Yara tav to take some action—not simply to find out, but to do something about the situation. This sounds much more like 1870-1872 than 1866-1867.

---

[52] Ralph H. Ogle, *Federal Control of the Western Apaches, 1848-1886* (Albuquerque, 1940), p. 62.

[53] Ibid. It is moot who made the first move, and quite probable that the Indians had been compelled to lay down any arms they could not easily conceal, before advancing to the parley.

The next incident is an utter mystery to me. Yara tav is supposed to have enticed some thirty to forty Yavapai men in to the Colorado River, where soldiers first fed them and then killed them all. The Yavapai chief named here I have not identified. The only record in accord with this narrative comes in a very general way indeed, through the Yavapai Michael Burns' report that "at least" three different parties of Yavapai had been brought to the Colorado River and "never returned" from there—and that they had been persuaded to come by promise of rations, clothing, and all kinds of presents.

It seems unwise to set aside such positive statements, one from each tribe supposed to have been involved. Whatever may have been lost from the memory of Chooksa homar by the time he told his story in 1903, he shows no signs of having embroidered events anywhere in his narrative, much less of having invented anything out of whole cloth. I see two possibilities: that he repeated in good faith a circumstantial but baseless story told him by someone else; or, just possibly, that this incident corresponds with the ambush of Quashackama at La Paz, on September 25, 1868.

Quashackama had for years been welcomed by whites on and near the reservation. He and his small band had managed to come and go between the reservation and his home in the interior, in spite of repeated policies on the part of the army to keep any Indian permanently on reservation once he came in for the first time. This West Yavapai band chief had done a great deal of useful service for the Indian agents, as a go-between, dealing with other bands and small groups that trailed in to the reservation at any season and without warning. The small business people in La Paz, south of the reservation proper, knew this man and esteemed him.

In spite of that, a group of freighters ambushed and killed Quashackama and from eight to fifteen of his companion Yavapai, just outside La Paz. No soldiers were involved. There were no military people there at the time, a small detachment having been withdrawn not long before. The army at once ordered a small company back to the vicinity, since the military officers were quite scandalized by this incident as were the Indian agent and business people in La Paz. The army detachment, although redundant so far as Indian-fighting was concerned, was maintained there through 1872 and later, in what seems to have been an attempt to make sure that such wanton aggression by whites would not recur. Since there was an attempt at the time by people at Prescott, who were interested in pressing the Indian war, to make out that Quashackama was a leading guerrilla and deserved a dog's death, it may be well to quote his only recorded words. He spoke in 1867 in answer to the question: Should Mohave and Chemehuevi now make peace? Said he, "I like the Americans, the Mexicans, the Yumas, the Chemehuevis, all the Indians—I don't want to fight anybody—I want peace all the time."[54]

The interval that follows does not help us to work our way into the white man's dating system. Yavapai and Walapai fought in the mountains, and soldiers went out against them in noticeably increased intensity in 1865; but in 1867 and 1868

---

[54] In the transcript of the prepeace conference meeting at the Colorado River Reservation, Feb. 11, 1867, in 734. The conference itself is mentioned in connection with the next episode, War with the Chemehuevi.

much more so, and of this period Ogle says that "Indian hostility now became widespread."[55] There were other bursts of such activity during spring and summer, 1869, and during the final push by General Crook's flying columns in late 1872. The most likely time for this interval in Chooksa homar's narrative would be fall and winter of 1868, but the whole proposition is too uncertain.

The unidentified ambush of Yavapai we discussed above could have occurred in 1865, or 1870, 1866 or 1872, as an eccentric event without discernible relationship to the general trends. The fact is that very few people, in that part of Arizona during those years, were living "under orders" of anyone else, or respecting anyone's policies.

To illustrate the instability of the situation even as early as 1865, one could inspect the relationships between Yara tav and his good friend and ally, Quashackama of the Yavapai and two associated "captains," Potamkay and Ah-hotch-a-cama. It is quite likely that these men had known each other before the 1860s. Yara tav was already seen as protector of one small group of Yavapai—probably Quashackama's own band—as early as 1863.[56] But there had always been some uneasiness, in Yara tav's view, of Yavapai coming to the Colorado River lowlands. Sometimes we can guess that it was the particular band or individuals he did not want with him;[57] and as time went on other reasons must have become as important. More Yavapai came, what with the pressure against their home ranges by whites, and knowing that food was distributed on the reservation.

Probably most important to the adverse shift in Mohaves' feelings, however, was the increasing tendency of Colorado River whites to use Yara tav and other leading figures among the Indians, first as go-betweens with the tribes in the interior, then as guides and spies against the same Yavapai and Walapai bands. Whereas Yara tav had been used at first only as a herald, to carry the invitation to Walapai and Yavapai to come in and settle on the River Reservation,[58] as the war brought more destruction to the property and optimism of the white settlers, Indian agents were more inclined to use friendly chiefs as apparatus of war against those other Indians presumed to be "hostile." By early 1867 this was the case;[59] and in 1868 Agent Helenus Dodt was able to compel Yara tav to still more slavish and aggressive actions against the reservation Yavapai, the result being

---

[55] *Federal Control of the Western Apaches,* pp. 72 ff.

[56] Conner, p. 87. It will be remembered that Quashackama signed the Fort Yuma treaty in April 1863. I see him receiving goods at the River Reservation as early as May 1865: Abstract of Goods Delivered to the [Indians on the Reservation], May 20, 1865, in 734.

[57] Weaver's notes to Charles Poston, from Prescott, Oct. 13, 1864, and Walnut Grove, Oct. 30, 1864, reporting that Yara tav would not welcome Yavapai from that part of the country.

[58] Feudge to Leihy, Sept. 5, 1866, in 734, and Leihy to the Commissioner of Indian Affairs, La Paz, Oct. 2, 1866, *Report, Indian Affairs,* 1867, p. 152, mentioning two such missions by Yara tav.

[59] Supt. Dent to the Commissioner, La Paz, Jan. 9, 1867, in 734, and *Weekly Arizona Miner,* May 4 and June 12, 1867, discussing two missions (to discover Leihy's murderers and report their identities; and to guide a pursuit of Walapais who had raided along lower Williams Fork). See agreement among nineteen "Contractors, Freighters, and Teamers, and Quashackama, Potamkay, and Meyace toomah (Yavapais)," La Paz, Aug. 27, 1868, that the Yavapai leaders would warn these whites of the approach of hostile Indians and "assist them to fight such hostile tribes," etc.; in 234. The best known of these whites were Julius Goldwater and Manuel Ravena. Capt. G. W. Davis' letter, Camp McPherson, Sept. 30, 1868, speaks of a recent whites' foray against Pinal Apaches, led by Quashackama himself; in Camp Date Creek, Letters Sent, 1868, in 393.

that Yara tav and other Mohave were forced into killing some of these Indians on the reservation, so as to prove to Dodt that the Mohave had had no part in recent thefts and depredations.[60] And there was further trouble between Mohave and Yavapai on the reservation the following year.[61] With the constant worry whether there would be enough food to go around to all Indians present, and with the pressing need to convince white officials of one's loyalty—or not receive that food—it was but a step to the final incident discussed below, with which this narrative of Walapai-Yavapai war concludes. Still, it is hard to know when any one enticement of Yavapai, to be murdered in cold blood by troops, could have occurred without a storm of protest from those whites who believed in fair treatment for Indians.

As for the next incident, in which Mohave acted as scouts for the United States Army, and Asukit pursued some Yavapai refugees to Yuma, I suspect that these two items were separated in time by several years. Certainly Major William R. Price was using Mohave scouts against the Walapai in mid-1867[62] and from then on.

The latter episode involves Asukit going to Yuma in pursuit of Yavapai who had taken refuge there, and ends with the confinement of Chemehuevi-hand on the Colorado River Reservation. My guess is that the narrator gives us here what should be the last incident in this group of ten: namely, the flight of a band leader and some of his people, during General Crook's final pursuit of all Yavapai bands without mercy or delay during 1872 and early 1873. Some of the bands ran for the hills and fought until they had lost most of their men. Others came to the reservations Crook had designated. The particular group mentioned here, led by Chemehuevi-hand, or Chumwavasal as he was also known, "did not want to fight, if fighting could be avoided, but did not care much for the new white neighbors whom they saw crowding in upon them," in the words of Crook's aide-de-camp, Lieutenant John G. Bourke.[63] Chemehuevi-hand and about one hundred fifty Yavapai left the Date Creek area and trekked down toward a hoped-for refuge among the Cocopa, according to Bourke. From what traces I have found of the halloo and pursuit of this group, Chemehuevi-hand probably was caught at last and lodged temporarily on the River Reservation.[64] Two years later he was brought back with other Yavapai and placed on another reservation.

---

[60] Supt. Geo. Andrews to Commissioner, Arizona City, Nov. 9, 1869, in 234.

[61] Andrews, Arizona City, Sept. 6, 1870, in *Report, Indian Affairs, 1870,* p. 116.

[62] Price, Fort Mohave, July 20, 1867, in *Walapai Papers,* p. 44. Henry L. Dobyns, "The Middle Mountain People" (mimeo., 1957), pp. 39-40, feels that another such case of a Mohave scouting for Price is seen in the attack on the Cerbat Mountain band, Jan. 14, 1868. Price reported again, at Camp Mohave, Sept. 25, 1868, that he had taken three Mohaves along as "runners and interpreters," and two Walapais: *Walapai Papers,* p. 73.

In an essay in *Proceedings of the American Philosophical Society,* 109 (June, 1965), I mentioned but two stages of Mohave dependence after 1859. Now I think of three, as seen in Yara tav's public acts: (a) sustained independent negotiations with whites and other tribes, 1859-65; (b) acting as herald of white policy and go-between with other tribes, 1865-67; (c) confederate in the whites' war against Indians, 1867-1873. But Yara tav was an exceptional person who kept trying to break the narrowing circle, as seen in his attempt at general peace in 1870 (below).

[63] *On the Border with Crook* (Columbus, Ohio, 1950: orig. publ. at New York, 1891), p. 171.

[64] Bourke says that Capt. James Burns pursued and brought the group in without bloodshed; but I can't be sure it was this group. Supt. Bendell wrote from Prescott, March 7, 1873, that Chemehuevi-Sal should be confined on the reservation whenever hands could be laid upon him. *The*

The next incident seems out of its chronological order but it is identifiable. Some of the westernmost Walapai bands had long been accustomed to coming to the Colorado River to farm the bottom land or to gather food; and from time to time between 1863 and 1873 there are mentions of their presence near Fort Mohave for longer or shorter periods of time. The incident recounted here seems to have been a known case of retaliation, not directed against certain offenders but simply against the most available Walapai; and it occurred September 23, 1866. The accounts all differ in detail, but they agree that a number of murders of white miners by Walapai brought a response by about ten white men accompanied by a considerable number of Mohave led by Homose-quahote and Asukit. The commandant of Fort Mohave, Captain Robert H. Porter, may have accompanied this foray, and he probably furnished supplies and pack animals for another such expedition, very soon afterward.[65] Needless to say, the Walapai account, if we had one, would no doubt begin with some aggression against them, rather than as I commenced the story above.

One of the accounts indicates that the two Mohave leaders of this raid had volunteered their services so as to entrench themselves in the good opinion of the whites, meaning not only with military officers but with miners, storekeepers, and others who lived close by Fort Mohave.

The final incident in this group of ten occurred in September 1872, at Camp Date Creek. It was a semiabortive attempt by General Crook to accomplish several things at once. He wanted to bring together chiefs and head men of the Yavapai to convince them to go to live on reservations. He was offering them a last chance just before his troops would move out all over that part of the country. Crook also believed his guests would include some of the same people who had ambushed the stagecoach near Wickenburg (November 5, 1871: the so-called "Loring Party" ambush). So he would take the opportunity of their presence in camp to snap them into jail. In the bargain, Crook thought that one of the Yavapai chiefs, Ochocama, was one of the murderers of Superintendent George Leihy, in 1866, and that man too would be bagged at the Date Creek conference.

But, as often happened, many of the Indians thought better of coming in at all. Only about fifty were present for the conference with Crook: and when Yara tav had handed out the plugs of tobacco, and guards started to lay hands on the wanted men, a free-for-all ensued. Chief Ochocama was imprisoned but at once escaped to the hills, seriously wounded; and within a very short time all of the Indians present were either out of sight or in jail. As Crook said, "My plan was to open the campaign by capturing the guilty parties";[66] so, having missed most of them he went ahead with the military phase of the campaign at once. Within a

---

Weekly Arizona Miner, March 29, 1873, speaks of a group of Indians going to the Colorado River at Ehrenberg and down river from there. Capt. MacGowan at Fort Yuma reported, April 26, that Chemehuevi-Sal and "disaffected" Yavapai were nearby, and Crook ordered him, from Prescott May 6, to arrest this leader if possible and send him up to Ehrenberg for return to Prescott by June 1 (or, if too late for that, to leave him on the reservation). But Crook's telegrams of Dec. 8 and Dec. 23, 1873, show that some Yavapai were still sheltering among the Quechans. For all these items see Dept. of Arizona, manuscript Letters Sent, 1873, in 393. Asukit is not mentioned.

[65] Agent Feudge to Commissioner of Indian Affairs, La Paz, Oct. 16, 1866, in 234; *Weekly Arizona Miner*, Oct. 13 and Nov. 10, 1866.

[66] Crook, *General George Crook, His Autobiography* (Norman, Okla., 1946), p. 174.

few months the guerrilla war against whites, and the United States Army war against Indians, were over and done with in that part of Arizona.

The other war, the gradual degradation and impoverishment, murder, and dispossession of Indians that had been going on ever since the first whites appeared, that was not yet finished by 1873. The history of that longer and much more fatal war is yet to be written.

Episode 12. War with the Chemehuevi

Having carried through with his remembrance of Walapai and Yavapai hostilities, the narrator begins all over again with the Chemehuevi. In so doing he drops back from 1873 into early 1865, to mention the pair of murders in Mohave Valley with which these hostilities began. Why this feud commenced, we do not learn.

A most important feature of this account is that the narrator was much more aware of events that occurred in Mohave Valley itself, or that originated or returned there. To put this more accurately, by comparing his account with other source material we can see that he did remember the incidents that occurred in the valley. He has more detail concerning these events, detail often not matched in the whites' records of the same happenings. But the whites' records include several incidents outside Mohave Valley that Chooksa homar does not so much as mention. Did he know of these more distant events at the time? Or did he never hear of them at all? These are important questions for anyone who concerns himself with oral history and the use of oral documents like the one we are examining. At this stage I can raise the questions but cannot provide satisfactory answers.

It would indeed be important to know whether in this reminiscence we see the shape of Chooksa homar's memory of things, or whether he was consciously omitting some kinds of events. I see three obvious reasons why this account of Chemehuevi hostilities might not include all the events that are there in the records. The narrator may never have heard, then or later, of some of the smaller cases of hostilities. Or, in 1903 his memory did not retain all he had been aware of during the late 1860s. Or, in 1903 he was consciously suppressing some events he could still remember. Inside this third possibility I suppose there could be at least two likelihoods: one, that he would omit some items because A. L. Kroeber had asked him to speak only to the one subject, war; or, that as a Mohave of his generation he would not feel free to mention certain facts to an outsider. I do not see how we can know, at this distance from the events and the narrator himself, which of these or other possibilities was the case.

No doubt we can find suggestive patterns—suggestions of omission, grouping of quotations, richness or sparsity of detail here and there. I have not tried to make these sorts of analyses for this purpose. It seems to me that we already have two kinds of narration included in the one reminiscence, and that for neither do we have abundant enough material with which to work.

That is, only some of the episodes in this narrative represent events that Chooksa homar himself witnessed. The others he reports from what he was told.

And my guess is that this double standard brings in unseen variables as to what Chooksa homar could remember, did remember, and would or would not say.

As for the very beginning of these hostilities with the Chemehuevi, one important element deserves mention although it cannot be proved. It is this: Chemehuevi and other Paiute bands were embroiled with the whites before they ever commenced hostilities with the Mohave. And from time to time there is the suggestion that the Chemehuevi resented Mohaves' friendly association with the military and other white men around Fort Mohave. This may give us one of only two reasons I can think of for these Mohave-Chemehuevi troubles. The Chemehuevi may have been saying, in effect, "join us against these white intruders or take the consequences." I have been unable to find enough good information on this to put it forward as a strong probability.

Another possibility and an especially good one in this case is that the Chemehuevi nation, like all other nations and tribes in that region, contained some who were inclined to associate with whites and some who drew away; some inclined to remain at peace with neighbors and others not so inclined. In this case it may well be that small bands of Chemehuevi followed one policy or the other. This would be very difficult to trace because the Paiute subdivisions were tiny, far-ranging, and seldom recorded by name of band, lineage, or chief. Let us copy here what Peter R. Brady wrote while serving as post interpreter at Fort Mohave in 1860, discussing the Paiutes, of whom he already had guessed that the Chemehuevi were but " a branch": "They seldom come into the Post in numbers of more than six or eight, and but upon one occasion have a larger number of them been here; it was over a month ago when they held a grand talk and at that time there were not over twenty or thirty."

It may well be, then, that the Chemehuevi leader most often mentioned by the whites, As-pan-ku-yah as Brady called him, was inclined to keep good relations or to restore them when once broken. He "lived in on the river" in 1860, Brady said; and he had been present at the peace-making with Major Armistead in 1859. He signed the Fort Yuma treaty in 1863, and received government food on the River Reservation at various times. I have no evidence that he ever went to war against any whites; and he was attempting to have his people allowed to come to the River Reservation in 1867. Again, my assumption about As-pan-kuh-yah is that although he happens to be one Chemehuevi who does appear often in the records, his behavior may not have been at all typical of the leading Chemehuevi then confronting both Mohave and white men, from the early 1860s until 1870.[67]

One other possible reason for these hostilities would be very hard to prove, but still quite likely: namely, that these troubles were based in the kind of relationship the Mohave had had, earlier, with Halyikwamai, Kohuana, and Halchidhoma residents along the Colorado. A. L. Kroeber had thoughts on this score although he never wrote about it at great length. He was thinking of the fact that the Mohave had tolerated these other, smaller tribes, in lands they continued to think of as their own. Then, they eventually drove these others out

---

[67] For general background of Chemehuevi life and their place among the Paiute, see Isabel Kelly, "Southern Paiute Bands," *American Anthropologist*, 36 (1934), 548 ff. The chief mentioned above was ordinarily named Pan Coyer, or Espanqua, by whites.

after long periods of coexistence, toleration, patronage, or sponsorship. The period when those earlier residents finally took flight from the Colorado River was believed by Leslie Spier to have been between 1825 and 1839; later, he thought between 1825 and 1830; and Kroeber after restudying Colorado River history early in the 1950s believed that 1828 was the most likely date.[68] In this view of things, the time simply came in the year 1865 when the Mohave no longer saw the Chemehuevi as pleasant enough cohabitants on the river, but began to look upon them as encroachers who must be sent on their way.

But with the Chemehuevi things worked out very differently than with those earlier tribes that had shared the Colorado lowlands with the Mohave. These Paiute were too numerous simply to be outnumbered and ejected in one or two campaigns. More importantly, they were accustomed to living in and traveling widely across the deserts, and were not anchored to a farming existence on the riverbanks. As fighters the bigger Mohave with their war clubs would beat them in a stand-up fight in the lowlands, but had poor luck in trying to pursue into the canyons and mountainsides above. There small groups of Chemehuevi would turn on them and inflict casualties, as we see in this present episode.

In any case, before 1865 the Mohave do not seem to have considered these Paiute as traditional enemies against whom they would aim their long, overland expeditions. When in 1859 Major Hoffman arrived at the western edge of Mohave Valley he found Paiute-Chemehuevi camped nearby. Earlier, we saw that the Chemehuevi gathered with the Mohave at the coming of the emigrant train in 1858. As A. L. Kroeber explained the relationship:

Up to 1858 the Chemehuevi on and near the Colorado, and the Mohave, did not intermingle, but rather, though there is no record of embroilments, kept themselves fairly separate. This was the easier in that all Chemehuevi farming settlements were on the California side of the river, whereas the Mohave downriver from their own ancestral valley, below the mouth of Bill Williams Fork where Parker Dam is now, preferred the wide valley and flood plain on the eastern side. There is no doubt that the Mohave regarded both sides of the valley as theirs by conquest from the Halchidhoma, as far down as at least La Paz, and as belonging, from about Blythe down, to the Yuma as their allies in this conquest. But they let their friends the Chemehuevi drift in from the desert and settle down and farm along the river in spots which none of themselves happened to be using.

More and more this sort of infiltration became established by usage, without the Mohave sensing that continued occupancy might ultimately cloud their title, which they had no intention of relinquishing. They owned a surplus, they liked being generous, they permitted use of land to their poorer neighbors, sometimes apparently invited them to use it. This is the meaning of their own statement . . . that 'they themselves brought the Chemehuevi to Cottonwood Island, where the two nations lived side by side, to Chemehuevi Valley, and to other points' [quoting his *Handbook of California Indians,* p. 594]; and, again, after the Halchidhoma defeat, 'the Chemehuevi began to drift into the valley now named after them'; after which the Mohave 'came in numbers, and by persuasion or compulsion induced the Chemehuevi to remove to Cottonwood Island at their northern limit' [*Handbook,* pp. 726-727]. This was somewhat as when they were ousting the Halchidhoma, they came, alleging friendship, to the other remnant tribe in the region, the Kohwana, and took them back north and kept them in Mohave Valley among themselves, as hostages or guests or as "pets," for five years before they allowed them to go off again [*Handbook,* pp. 800-801].

However, in 1859 the Mohave were defeated in their home valley by American troops; and as their fortunes declined, those of the hitherto tolerated or patronized Chemehuevi rose in contrast. By about 1865 open war broke out between the two tribes, and was carried on with bitterness. Each side alleged

---

[68] Spier, *Cultural Relations of the Gila and Lower Colorado River Tribes* (New Haven, 1936), p. 3; Kroeber, notes to the present ms.

that the other began with some wanton murders; nothing is said about land; encroachments may have been an underlying factor . . . .[69]

So now suddenly there was war. And for five years this became an oppressive, fearful situation for the Mohave. They were now divided, some living near the fort and others on the River Reservation. They could be attacked in detail and perhaps scattered into the desert. They were especially vulnerable to an enemy living nearby who knew exactly the yearly round of their life, and who observed their comings and goings at close range. Nor was there any prospect of a reunion of the Mohave nation or a concentration of its people, either near the fort or on the reservation.

To the Fort Mojave Indians the issue was, as Lorraine Sherer puts it, land—to hold to the ancestral home, its farmlands, its deep associations with traditional usage and tribal memory. To those who had moved southward, the point was to find a brighter future with the Indian agent's bounty, and with the promise of large-scale and reliable annual farming by means of a long irrigation canal let into the Colorado River. The struggle over the question of where to live turned to some extent on the resolve of Homose-quahote in the north and Yara tav in the south.

After 1865 the tension between the two groups of Mohave was complicated by the whites in local authority, Indian agents in the south and post commanders in the north, each abetted by other whites with property and business interests and local viewpoints. It is hard to see how the "divided house of the Mohave" could have been reconciled in any case; but the influence of white people seems to have hurried matters into a permanent alienation of the two tribal factions. In late 1866 the commandant of Fort Mohave had taken some action to restore Homose-quahote to his dignity of Great Chieftain, relinquished some years before; but the Indian agent at Parker, with strong local backing, was loud and persistent in resisting such a change.[70] In an important sense, both Indian leaders were bound by these actions of white men influential in their neighborhoods, whether or not they might have worked out an accommodation if left to themselves.

The more serious outcome, thinking of the hostilities with the Chemehuevi, was that each division of the Mohave felt too weak to confront a major attack. Each tended to take refuge near the whites—at the agency, or under protection of the fort—and the commandant and agent often accentuated the tribal division and dependence rather than trying to restore tribal unity. While this war was still

---

[69] A. L. Kroeber, ms. "Chemehuevi-Mohave Relations, 1859-1867," prepared for use in Dockets 88, 283, 295, 319-320, 330, 351, claims cases before the Indian Claims Commission. Docket 351 comprises The Chemehuevi Tribe of Indians, The Chemehuevi Tribe of Indians by Dan Eddy, Petitioners, vs. United States of America, Defendant; in USNA.

[70] Sherer, "Great Chieftains," pp. 8-14, by close reading of the documents has shown how the title of Great Chieftain shifted back to Homose-quahote in 1867. I infer that this was precipitated or formalized in some one action of the commandant. Supt. Dent's letter to the commandant, Major Richard Porter, Jan. 27, 1867, spoke slurringly of "some other Indian" having been given the chieftain's title recently held by Yara tav. See also Citizens of La Paz to Dent, Jan. 22, 1867; and Dent's very large, elaborate good-conduct passport to Yara tav, Jan. 1, 1867, styling him "Head Chief" of the Mojave Indians; all in 734. See plate 2.

continuing it finally became clear that Homose-quahote would not settle wherever Yara tav might be. All this meant still further dependence upon the whites, as the Mohave in the valley and those near Parker time and again left their crops untended because of rumors of attack from across the river.

Chooksa homar's narrative does not make apparent one factor of importance in the situation: the attitude of the whites toward the Chemehuevi. One might expect that these people—storekeepers, army officers, Indian agents, freighters, miners—would side with the Mohave and might even join them against the Paiute.

But no such thing occurred. When more troops became available in western Arizona in early fall of 1867, these operated to the eastward, not westerly or northward into Paiute country. Presumably the objective was to protect miners and transportation routes leading to central Arizona and to the territorial capital, Prescott. By late 1867 Colonel William Price, as part of his intensive war on the Walapai, plotted to bring the Chemehuevi-Paiute into direct hostility with the Walapai. He planned to bring these Paiute to the Colorado River Reservation later on.[71]

This meant that the Paiute were dealt with by one group of soldiers working from posts north and west of Mohave Valley. Meanwhile the Walapai and Yavapai were the target of soldiers who occupied other army camps and posts, the westernmost of which was Fort Mohave. What seems today an anomaly disturbed none of the army officers then: so Fort Mohave was often the resort of Paiute and Chemehuevi who visited peaceably there, even though their congeners and perhaps they themselves were conducting guerrilla war against the whites, beginning just out of sight of the fort.

Something like this situation obtained also in the south. Chemehuevi came and went from the town of La Paz and nearby settlements, and did casual labor on nearby ranches, without anyone concerning themselves—if indeed most of the whites understood—that this same tribe was, just a few days' foot travel away, in a state of war against both whites and Mohave. Where the Chemehuevi were mentioned in citizens' petitions, as undesirables, the objection was to their hostilities east of the Colorado River and was not directed at the desert war to the westward.

For the first incident in this chronicle of Chemehuevi-Mohave war, the attacks in Cottonwood and Chemehuevi valleys, all we need say is that the northern of these two does appear in the whites' records and the southern one does not. The details of both seem to ring true to what is known of the situation and participants. The presence of Yavapai allies in the Chemehuevi Valley affair accords with what the Yavapai later told Edward Gifford about their traditional enmities.

We lose control of any sure chronology as soon as these attacks are past. Did the large number of Chemehuevi leave the Colorado River in 1865, and stay away in Southern California for several years thereafter? This has been a tradition, and A. L. Kroeber later discovered that some refugees had stayed permanently among the Cahuilla, having arrived among them at some time in the late 1860s.[72]

[71] Price's report, Jan. 1868, *Walapai Papers*, p. 62.
[72] *Ethnography of the Cahuilla Indians*, UCPAAE, 8 (June, 1908), 32, 37.

But the reports of Indian agents on the Colorado continue to mention Chemehuevi during 1866 and 1867. Their only real absence from those records came during summer and fall of 1866, partly caused by exceptionally high waters on the river which impeded travel. My guess is that some Chemehuevi became refugees in 1865, but that others remained closer at hand, unnoticed because they lived and moved in such small groups and customarily concealed themselves, out of sight of the river lowlands.

The best we can do is to guess that the Chemehuevi attack into Mohave Valley, which Chooksa homar says ended with five Mohave dead, was the same as occurred about mid-June 1866, and was reported to Agent John Feudge on the River Reservation. But the chronology cannot be very reliable when neither the Mohave's narrative nor the whites' reports mention all the same incidents, or when there is some doubt of the accuracy of some information the whites received.

The early months of 1866 give us good illustration of the confusion in this picture. Superintendent Leihy reported that a small settlement of Indians in Mohave Valley had been attacked in mid-March,[73] and twenty-five Mohave killed. Then on June 23, according to Agent Feudge, two Chemehuevi were killed near La Paz, having crossed the river at Bradshaw's Ferry six miles below. One of the Mohave chiefs on the reservation then informed Feudge of an attack in Mohave Valley, by Chemehuevis who had crossed the Colorado and killed four Mohave. Opposite these reports to the whites, Chooksa homar mentions but one incident, one in which five Mohave were killed. But he emphasized that it had been twenty-five Mohave who bravely fought off the attackers, the whole day through. My feeling is that there are not enough firm indications to justify pairing any one report by the whites with the one incident Chooksa homar describes.

Next we come to an interval between battles, when the narrator says that the Chemehuevi returned to the valley bearing their name. My guess is that this occurred just after the campaign of thirty-two days carried out against Indians in Southern California, outward from San Bernardino.[74] That campaign resulted in pushing some of the desert Indians away from the white settlements, and I assume that some of the Chemehuevi came back to the river at that time, probably during February 1867.

There is one other possible reason why the Chemehuevi might have come back to their valley in early 1867. Superintendent George Dent of the Colorado River Reservation was interested in bringing those people within the reservation's orbit, knowing as he did that the Chemehuevi had been more or less orphaned by the Office of Indian Affairs. That is, they figured bureaucratically as California Indians and were therefore not budgeted for food on the River Reservation. But they were too far from the California superintendent at San Francisco, or the agent at Los Angeles, to receive attentions from them. So in January 1867, Dent sent out a messenger to talk with the chief of the Chemehuevi about a peace conference with the Mohave.

---

[73] Leihy to Agent J. Q. A. Stanley, March 21, 1866, and his quarterly report to the commissioner, done in early April, both in 734; and *Weekly Arizona Miner,* May 9, 1866.

[74] Beattie and Beattie, *Heritage of the Valley,* pp. 420-421, and a brief remark by Michael Goldwater of La Paz, in *Alta California [APHS transcript],* Feb. 9, 1867.

Dent meanwhile held a conference with Mohave and Yavapai chiefs on the reservation to ensure their cooperation; and in March he sponsored a treaty between Mohaves and Chemehuevis. Although this agreement did not end the war, it may well have impelled some of the Chemehuevi refugees in California to return to the Colorado River where one of their leading men, As-pan-ku-yah, wanted to live.[75]

I am the more inclined to think of the return of some Chemehuevi as occurring in early 1867, by the tenor of what comes next in Chooksa homar's narrative. Although the battle he discusses, a Mohave attack into Chemehuevi Valley, was not reported to the whites, the whole trend of events sounds right for 1867 and on into 1868. The Chemehuevi had come back along the river, although they moved cautiously there and almost imperceptibly. When bloodied in Chemehuevi Valley, some of them moved down close to the reservation itself, to which point Dent had been trying to attract them. Certainly they were back in that neighborhood, near La Paz, by April 1867,[76] and whereas the Indian agents had not noticed any Chemehuevi at all during the latter half of 1866 or January 1867, there are mentions of them after that. Yara tav said, at the February prepeace meeting, that a Chemehuevi had visited him recently and sounded him out about a return of the tribe to the Colorado River. By May, Agent Stanley at Los Angeles was writing to Arizona on the obvious assumption that some Chemehuevi were already on the Colorado and in need of food.[77]

If they were there, but very few and keeping out of the way of the Mohave and the reservation whites most of the time, we can guess that the events Chooksa homar next describes—a Mohave attack against Chemehuevi, near Parker, with five Chemehuevi killed—more likely occurred in 1869. For 1868 no hostilities at all were reported in the agent's letters. But in 1869 a traveling military inspector, who had known the country earlier, reported some Chemehuevi on the west bank of the Colorado above La Paz.[78]

The next two incidents in the narrative, attacks by Mohave near Parker and

---

[75] In 734: Isaac Bradshaw to Dent, Cotton Wood Slough, Feb. 2, 1867; Agent J. Q. A. Stanley to Dent, Los Angeles, Feb. 11, 1867; transcript of Mohave-Yavapai meeting with Dent on Feb. 11, Yara tav, Mockneil, and Tomas speaking for the Mohave, Quashackama for Yavapai; Dent's letters, Feb. 27 to Stanley, and Feb. 13, April 1, and March 1, 1867, to the Commissioner. The treaty is enclosed in his April 1 letter, to be found in 234.

[76] Resolutions adopted by "all the Miners and Settlers resident at Planet, Great Central and Springfield Mining Companies on Williams Fork in Arizona": at Planet Camp, April 18, 1867, in 734.

[77] J. Q. A. Stanley to Dent, Los Angeles, May 25, 1867, in 734. Supt. B. C. Whiting of California wrote from San Francisco May 25, 1867, that he had already furnished seed to Chemehuevi for that year's planting (Records of the Adjutant General's Office, Letters Received, Main Series, 1861-1870, AGO); but I doubt he could have acted so speedily, since his agent at Los Angeles had written but two weeks earlier that there would be no supplies for the Chemehuevi that year from California. Chemehuevi were involved in the ambush of the Yavapai chief, Quashackama, near La Paz, in September 1868. I am assuming, then, that some Chemehuevi were living, carefully and watchfully, on the California bank of the Colorado after early 1867.

[78] Lt.-Col. Roger Jones' letter, San Francisco, July 21, 1869, in *Report, Indian Affairs, 1870*, p. 216. Supt. Dent had found 200 Paiute near Fort Mohave in January, and said that "I have ever invited them to come to the Colorado Reservation and live there"; from La Paz, to the Commissioner, Jan. 2, 1869, in 734. Col. Jones stated that Chemehuevi were occasionally receiving supplies from the agent at the reservation, and some flour from the army at the fort.

then into Chemehuevi Valley, seem likely to have occurred during 1869 or early 1870. From late 1869 Agent Dodt kept reporting a nervousness among the reservation Indians. He never did figure out what was causing this feeling, and he supposed that it promised some sort of alliance between Mohave and Maricopa, with a probable move of reservation Mohave to the Gila River. He was right in that the Maricopa and Mohave leaders were trying to promote an Indian peace throughout western Arizona. But I think we can assume that the nervousness and fear Dodt noticed were caused by the near presence of the Chemehuevi and by the recent resumption of conflict with them.

The first move of Chemehuevi on to the land of the reservation that I can find in the records occurred in May 1870;[79] and, following dates in the whites' records, the final hostilities between the two nations began only two months later, in the vicinity of Fort Mohave. This was followed in turn by the last battle, on October 15, 1870. Chooksa homar's account of that battle is more detailed than the whites' records I have seen, and they all agree closely on important points. Here again, Chooksa homar did not know of, or did not remember, some hostilities on the reservation, during mid-September and early October.[80]

As with the whole reminiscence, and as with this war of five years between tribes who had once coexisted peacefully, so in this final battle we see how the influence of the whites was everywhere penetrating the Indians' life. Some of these warriors bore white man's arms. A few whites were asked to take part, and the Mohave had long before that day begun to shelter under the white man's protection. When peace was made at last between Chemehuevi and Mohave it was through the white man's mediation. So ended a war fought on traditional lines but in the shade of conquest by tribes no longer free.

Episode 13. Acceptance of Law

This final episode very fittingly closes this narrative by bringing to the fore one kind of event, and one quality of relationship, into which Indian life in Arizona had already gradually been bent, and in which it would continue during the next generation and more. Where once the brave man, the kwanami, had but to dream of war and so to envisage and then to lead a new campaign against the tribal enemy, he had first been reduced to scouting and spying against those enemies, and now he had come to live out his days as an Indian policeman, keeping order among his own people or otherwise serving the white captain. All this must be done according to the white man's code of crime and justice.

In this instance many Chemehuevi were working for a company on the Blythe tract, digging a large irrigation ditch. For whatever reason, they had a grudge against the foreman-superintendent on the job, John Calloway. The Indian agent visiting the scene not long before had written that "I learn that there is a personal animosity felt toward the Superintendent Mr. Calloway and I believe he will ultimately be killed by them."[81]

---

[79] Dodt to Supt. Andrews, from the reservation, June 5, 1870, in 734.

[80] Dodt's letters of Sept. 19 and Oct. 19, in 734, reported a Chemehuevi attack on the reservation, September 17, and the murder of a Chemehuevi boy, just south of the reservation, on October 8.

[81] Henry Mallory to Commissioner, Jan. 31, 1880: Colorado River Reservation, Letters to Com-

The agent's account of the murder, heard from a mail carrier the day afterward, is very close to the Mohave narrator's version. This all happened on a Sunday payday with its round trip to Ehrenberg, coming home drunk and finding several of the white men strolling out after dinner. In the scuffle while Calloway was refusing entrance to the building, he was attacked from at least two directions and knifed to death.[82]

If the violence itself was over and done with on that day, March 28, and did not spread into hostilities on a larger scale, what had seemed regrettable and simple and small turned out nevertheless to be a near chaos. A month or six weeks went by while attempts were made to quiet the Indians; and the reports show that there was much more tension, and the prospect of large-scale fighting, before order was restored.

In hindsight, what impresses one so vividly is the multiplicity of authority that came into play, and the unmistakable demonstration that, as late as 1880, the only dampener was still a large enough number of troops. On April 4 arrived four Mohave, coming from the vicinity of Fort Mohave, and the first who attempted to adjust this matter. They were said by the agent to have included the tribal chief and two subordinate chiefs. One of these men, as we have seen in the narrative, was Asukit. But their authority, in one sense tribal and also in direct deputation of the commandant of Fort Mohave, was not accepted by the Chemehuevi. Nor is it clear that these men dared even to cross the river and talk directly with head men there. It looks as if any Indian mediation that was accomplished later on was by some reservation Mohave, not by these four from the fort.

The second authority to act was the Indian agent himself, but it was obvious to him very early in the going that the Chemehuevi considered him to be in league with the United States Army, which was sending a group of ten soldiers up from Yuma. Mr. Mallory was unable to do anything useful at all, and he came near leaving the agency with women and children, to get them out of harm's way. This was also a maneuver to shock some of the Mohave men into acting as an agency guard during the emergency, and this tactic did succeed.

Thus, when another authority, a young lieutenant serving as commandant of Fort Yuma, came with his ten soldiers or soon after them, and arriving at the agency probably between April 15 and April 18, he found that the agent had mobilized the Mohave guard. So Lieutenant Hyde had "20 Indian soldiers armed with bows and arrows, a few pistols and four old Spencer carbines—a Falstaffian crew . . . ."[83] But he also discovered how nervous the situation was. Even though Henry Mallory did arrange a conference with sixteen Chemehuevi at the agency, feelings were running so high that upon the agent's advice and his own best judgment, Lieutenant Hyde and his men did not show themselves at all

missioner, 1879-1917, Federal Records Center, Bell, California. Gen. O. B. Willcox, commanding the Department of Arizona, wrote from Prescott, Sept. 11, 1880, that "it was afterwards ascertained that Calloway was killed by the Chemijuevis in retaliation for having killed one of their tribe": *Report, War, 1880*, p. 208.

[82] Mallory to Commissioner, March 31, 1880, in the Federal Records Center file cited in n. 81, above.

[83] Lt. J. McE. Hyde to Dr. Jos. K. Corson, River Reservation, April 19, 1880 (I saw these Hyde letters by courtesy of Prof. B. Fontana, and use them by kind permission of Dr. Jos. K. Corson of Philadelphia).

while the Chemehuevi were present.[84] After the conference the Chemehuevi went off to ask for their jobs back at the company. This was refused unless they gave up the "guilty man" first; and Mallory concluded that "This affair is now entirely beyond any peace policy and has to be settled in the War Department, as it is unsafe for a White man or a Mohave Indian to cross the Colorado River at any place . . . ."[85] Lieutenant Hyde thought it "a question" whether the Chemehuevi would give up the murderer, and he wrote that there "will be no security here until they [the Chemehuevi] are well thrashed and disarmed."[86]

On the last day of April came two companies of United States infantry with other troops and supplies, and it seems that it was necessary for them to go all the way to Chemehuevi Valley in order to overawe the tribe still sheltering its man.[87]

So at last the presence of a truly overwhelming force of soldiers brought on the final negotiation and delivery of two murderers,[88] as is stated by Chooksa homar. And, although he does not say so, the United States government took this occasion to move these Chemehuevi north, to the Colorado River Reservation.[89]

Henry Mallory was the only participant whose conclusions I have seen: as for the Chemehuevi, "They are a hard tribe to manage, as they are very intelligent and brave." As for what had just passed, "The cause of this trouble was more from injudicious management by Mr. Calloway than anything else."[90] It does seem, from General Willcox's report after the whole affair was over with, and from Chooksa homar's narrative, as if Calloway had killed one of the Chemehuevi on the job and thus triggered his own murder.

I am not sure that any larger meanings were then seen, by Chooksa homar who was probably far from the scene, or by Mohave chiefs, army officers, or by any others in this little war of nerves. Today we would probably ask whether a single act of violence might serve to raise serious questions, especially where that single act then uncovers much more, many people willing to "do violence" to the codes so recently imposed on them and so foreign to their own way of life.

All of this is not to praise, or to excuse, or to locate blame. It is merely to recall that white men, through this generation of hostility in Arizona, so seldom recognized how partial and how biased were the thoughts they represented in the one word, "war." They had not understood that they were making constant war upon the Indians. Mostly, they failed to see that Indians insofar as possible had also been making war on whites. By 1880 they might all have known that when war ends there may not yet be peace.

---

[84] Hyde's letter of April 23, ibid.; Mallory's report of the same conference in his letter of April 23, in the Federal Records Center file cited in n. 81.

[85] Quoted in his letter of April 23; see also his letter of April 27, concerning the refusal to let the Chemehuevi go back to work; he had sent a Mohave chief and an interpreter along to help the Chemehuevi with this request.

[86] Hyde's letter of April 23, 1880.

[87] Hyde's letter of April 30, 1880. Mallory's annual report, August 1, 1880, *Report, Indian Affairs, 1880,* p. 124, is no doubt correct as to detail save for dates. He says March 8 for the murder, meaning March 28; and he says April 12 for the arrival of Col. Price and troops, whereas Hyde's date, April 30th at noon, fits the chronology. As nearly as I can tell from the few documents cited here, four companies of troops came, two with Price, two following him by a day or so.

[88] Hyde's letter of Sept. 11, 1913, says that the two were confined in the U.S. military prison on Alcatraz Island "for two or three years," rather than at San Quentin as in the Mohave text.

[89] Willcox's letter and Mallory's annual report, as cited above.

[90] In his annual report as cited above.

CONCLUSION

THE KWANAMI; AND DEFENSIVE AND OFFENSIVE WAR

Chooksa homar's narrative reenforces much that has been written and leaves some questions unanswered. The first episode, the attack on the Cocopa, best reflects the old-style offensive warfare. The kwanami, Yara tav, having dreamt of this campaign, led the Mohave expedition which culminated in seizure of captives and a traditional fiesta upon return to the valley. Even as late as during the war against the Chemehuevi we still see the traditional routines of offensive warfare: the attacks near Cottonwood Island and into Chemehuevi Valley, the stand-up battle near Parker, and the abortive expedition that found no enemies in Chemehuevi Valley. Insofar as we learn, all these were initiated by kwanami, and the fight near Parker shows the warriors staging one of their formal battles.

To the degree we see the kwanami in this narrative, they went to war as individuals rather than, as has been supposed, as a separate unit of warriors. Leslie Spier wrote as follows on this issue:

It would seem rather that some men received in dreams special power for war and gave their concern to it from boyhood, precisely as other appropriate dreams gave power and skill for other specialized pursuits. But that they formed a distinct class and were organized even but informally, is open to question in view of the non-occurrence of anything similar on record for adjacent Yuman tribes. It is, of course, conceivable that the Mohave emphasized the peculiar character of these men more than other culturally related tribes did, but the matter should be checked.[91]

For example, the battle near Parker was suggested by one kwanami and conducted under his aegis. On another occasion "it was decided" to attack the Chemehuevi, and word went throughout the tribe. We see head men and old men talking about what to do when the whites approach. At least, no association of kwanami is inferred by Chooksa homar.

As for defensive fighting, this was one of many aspects of Mohave culture that was soonest and most radically affected from 1859 onward, by white domination and by shifting relationships among nearby tribes. So far as we know, the Mohave had never felt themselves to be on the defensive before this; they had never lived apprehensively until that generation. So I do not assume that what Chooksa homar tells us of defensive war reflects purely aboriginal custom.

He tells us nothing of the highly formalized usages that have been reported by other Mohave narrators—guard patrols, spies keeping in touch with hostile tribes to give early warning of attack, or horses kept on station in Mohave Valley for the sole purpose of notifying tribesmen of coming invasion. As seen in this reminiscence, a number of raids penetrated the valley without warning, arguing against there having been any elaborate defenses at all. Still, there is that one interesting remark by Lieutenant Tuttle, who claimed to have seen a night-pa-

---

[91] Spier, *Mohave Culture Items* (Flagstaff, Ariz., 1955), p. 15. See Kenneth Stewart, "Mohave Warfare," *Southwestern Journal of Anthropology*, 3 (Summer, 1947), and George Fathauer, "The Structure and Causation of Mohave Warfare," ibid., 10 (Spring, 1954).

trol system in Mohave Valley.[92] Perhaps such a guard was maintained, as has been reported, only when a Mohave war party was out of the valley on an expedition.

As to why we hear nothing of a national defense system in Chooksa homar's memoir, it may be that Kroeber did not really want to hear about all that. I am guessing that Kroeber asked only for the eventful history, leaving aside for the time being all description of weapons, individuals' names and roles, paraphernalia, and ceremonies, that would give a more rounded view of Mohave war customs. This seems likely, because, if my memory serves me, Kroeber had very little time to hear this narrative (parts of two days); and, he was specifically interested in the war narrative as a form of Indian literature.

Another question arises as to who planned and who participated in war. Some have assumed that the call went to everyone in the nation, and that any man of fighting age might answer such a call. The exact opposite view is also reported: that offensive war was the province only of kwanami. They dreamed it, they carried it out, whether a small raid or one of the big expeditions in which the kwanami would be but a few of the many taking part. Common to both views is the conviction that most people had nothing to say about the coming of hostilities.

We should put this in the Mohave way: "Dreaming took the place of learning in the native view; all professional status and all success was achieved by dreams."[93] Either all able-bodied men could dream of war, or only the kwanami would do so. This in turn raises questions about dreaming and warfare, which I do not believe are to be answered in Chooksa homar's narrative, although I think we can see there an interplay that does concern decision-dreaming, or the "power-giving dream."

That is, Wallace supposes that the Mohave could see the future in two different kinds of dreams. The "power-giving" ones were major experiences, carrying the person backward in time into the presence of the originator of the nation, the culture hero Mastamxho, who foresaw what would occur. His was the authority conferring the knowledge, if necessary also the power, acquired by the dreamer's wandering spirit, and which the dreamer then carried back with him into waking life. But there were also simple dreams, which could come to a person much more frequently than was ever likely with the power-giving experience. These simpler dreams might merely shed light on immediate future events, either in direct narrative, or by appearance of symbols. Not everyone would have even one power-giving dream in his lifetime; almost anyone at any time might experience the simple dream.[94]

I think the question that has arisen among ethnographers, as to who planned war and who followed along on campaign, can only be answered by knowing

---

[92] E. D. Tuttle, "The River Colorado," *Arizona Historical Review*, 1 (1928), 50-68: see p. 59: the Mohave "maintained a regular line of pickets or police, up and down the valley. At daylight each patrol could be heard passing the word that all was well." He may be reporting from the year 1863, when he first ascended the river.

[93] Spier, "Cultural Relations," p. 6, in accord with all those who have participated in or observed Mohave life.

[94] William J. Wallace, "The Dream in Mohave Life," *Journal of American Folk-lore*, 60 (July-Sept., 1947), 252-254.

such a basic fact as whether a major expedition required some kwanami to report a power-giving dream; and, whether others would accompany him only if they had experienced a simple, ordinary dream which augured favorably for the expedition.

In the narrative it seems barely possible that we are seeing a struggle between the war and peace parties based on dream authority seen in the light of outcomes. That is, if an enterprise were to fail after a man had claimed that power "had been bestowed upon him he was looked upon as a charlatan and his dream was considered a fabrication: Public scorn and criticism were heaped upon him."[95] It looks possible that Yara tav's harping upon the war party's miscalculations and mistaken assumptions about the whites' power could represent Yara tav's attempt to heap public discredit upon those who had reported warlike dreams and then had seen their predictions fail.

This in turn suggests a question about multiple roles in warfare, especially the shamans' role. I see nothing in this narrative to add to the very slight information Spier and Kenneth Stewart had from their informants, who spoke of the shamans either as scalping, or as going along in a medical capacity. In 1874 one of the army officers reported that "medicine men" had much to do with initiating campaigns. Perhaps they had power-giving dreams more often than did others.

Yara tav's granddaughter reported that he had been a shaman,[96] in addition to his chieftainship and his role as a kwanami. We can look at his remark in this narrative, where he threatens the five kwanami at the end of the third episode, saying "I will somehow fix you." I do not believe that this signified putting a "hex" on the five kwanami, for to do that would constitute public admission of one's status as a witch, with the consequent and immediate danger of being killed by other tribesmen. And we can be very sure that, whether he was a shaman or not and whether as a shaman he also in time became a witch, no such thing was in his mind yet in 1859. His whole public career in its most difficult aspects still lay before him.

So, we can summarize the answers to questions about war leadership and war participation by saying that, as seen in this narrative, campaigns launched against tribal enemies were indeed dreamed by the kwanami, so far as we can tell. What relations there were between dreaming, and taking part in an expedition already proclaimed, we do not know. And as for formal behavior of Mohaves when under attack by other tribes, neither this narrative nor any other source I know of is clear. With so little information and with the chance of so many unseen variables, I would not care to speculate.

As for whether kwanamis could serve other roles as well, this narrative shows that they could. The narrator says, of the five brave men at Fort Yuma, that "They were all ranked evenly then: later on, some were intelligent and were ranked ahead and became chiefs." This could mean merely that white officers later appointed them as "captains," as the Fort Yuma commandant was doing at

[95] Ibid., pp. 253-254.

[96] Devereux, *Mohave Ethnopsychiatry and Suicide: the Psychiatric Knowledge and the Psychic Disturbances of an Indian Tribe* (Washington, D.C., 1963), p. 65, reporting Tcatc's information; and see his "Mohave Chieftainship in Action . . .," *Plateau*, 23 (Jan. 1951), 33-43, for a brief account of Yara tav and other matters, by Tcatc.

that very moment. But with what we know from Peter Brady's report of 1860, of those five kwanami two were already chiefs, two more became chiefs soon thereafter, and it is unlikely that the fifth man ever became a chief. One can guess that, the society being what it was, kwanami might well have been preferred for the quasi-hereditary chieftainships, over other men without warlike distinction.

THE NARRATOR'S FORMAL VIEWPOINT

Chooksa homar's own view of Mohave war was not based on a simple chronological view of things, nor on that form of it which sees together those events which occurred at the same time. His outlook seems to have been toward surrounding and impinging peoples, friends, enemies, and acquaintances. This is as static a viewpoint as one would expect for a man of his nation and of his generation within it. And I suspect that this accounts for his putting the Maricopa mission out of what I believe to be its chronological place. Having spoken of the Cocopa, what next comes to mind are the Gila River tribes who sided with the Cocopa against Quechan and Mohave; so the next episode after the Cocopa raid is the peace mission to the Maricopa.

We have commented already on what seems to be Chooksa homar's formalism in whatever involves time. I imagine that all his phrases for time are formalisms until we reach some action that is unfolding—especially if it were something with which Chooksa homar himself had been familiar, or some action he had carried out himself, like a trip across a desert or a battle in progress. And it looks as if this works out in detail. In recounting trips along the Colorado River which he must have known very well, his account of time not only "sounds right" to us, it was very close to the exact time needed for the trip. When he gives details of Yara tav's mission to the Maricopa, Chooksa homar falls back into formalisms again, because the country was not well known to him.

On the other hand we would not expect him to envision the whole span of time of this narrative as we would think of it, more or less 1854 to 1880. Not only did he lack the time-anchoring habit of our dating system,[97] but also he did not think of the intervals between incidents as we think of them. To Chooksa homar, obviously there was no need to be precise about all that. I am reminded that some day others will wonder at my own use of such phrases as "When this was all over and done with," or "A long time afterward," or "Later on."

In the narrator's statement of small numbers we probably see formalism part of the time but not always: when he says "one" or "two" he may mean just that. Where he says "five" I suspect it was only rarely four plus one, and probably signified "a few," or even "some" as we would put it. But as with so much else in this narrative the indications are too few to support conclusions.

Finally, many pertinent events occurred that are not mentioned by Chooksa homar: and I mean events of all the same kinds he does include—formal expeditions, small raids, defense against surprise attack, peace-making missions, and simple murder. But before mentioning examples of all those, let us remark on

---

[97] The Mohave calendar and habits of reckoning time within a given year are briefly discussed by Spier, *Mohave Culture Items,* pp. 16-17.

his freedom from taboo against naming persons recently dead. He observed no real prohibitions, either as to persons who had died just before 1903, or as to any Mohave he had known who had died long before. Just a few years before he gave this story to Quichnailk and Kroeber, two men prominent in his own lifetime and in the narrative had died, Asukit and Qolho qorau; yet they each have their proper place in the story. Yara tav's death is mentioned, interestingly enough "not so very long ago" when it had been twenty-nine years. The death of Avi-havasuts is discussed, whereas the name of one kwanami is given while he lives but not mentioned when he dies in battle against Armistead's men.

As for the long narrative concerning the Chemehuevi, Walapai, and Yavapai, I have already stated that Chooksa homar seems not to have been as alive to those events that occurred beyond his immediate view, that did not originate in or return to Mohave Valley. During these periods of hostilities involving other tribes, Mohaves were often involved. While Chooksa homar does give us one incident from the Walapai war, for instance, there were literally dozens of others. Mohave were involved first as casual friends of some Walapai, later on serving the army as go-betweens, and finally as collaborators, spies, and scouts with the army against some of the Walapai.

As a specific example of the kind of semi-warlike incident that Chooksa homar must have known well enough to narrate, the escape of Tokoomhet (Sherum, chief of the Cerbat Mountain band) stands out. This Walapai chief was brought to Fort Mohave under guard after a long career of sometimes hostile, sometimes complaisant relations with troops at Fort Mohave. This time he was to be taken to the San Francisco Bay region for confinement; but he evaded his guards and escaped, probably with some involvement of Asukit at every stage, Asukit being an old friend of Tokoomhet from years before.[98] We cannot say why such incidents as this one are not in Chooksa homar's narrative.

It is even harder to explain the absence of another incident from the year 1872, which so very closely resembles the Calloway episode that concludes this memoir. In September 1872 a great stir was caused among both whites and Mohaves when some tribesmen murdered one of a party of whites who were invading and using Mohave farm land without permission. The whites in the vicinity mustered a posse of more than a hundred men; and for their part the Mohave on one occasion came with almost three hundred ready to do battle.[99] The event was poignant beyond what we might easily understand today, because as of 1872 the Mohave living near the fort had no title whatsoever to their lands, and were in constant doubt as to their future in their own traditional homes.

As for peace-making missions, Chooksa homar does not tell us either of the Fort Yuma meeting of 1863, nor of the last and most ambitious effort involving the Mohave, in 1870. Shadowy although it may be in the available records, here was an attempt to make mutual peace arrangements among all the western

[98] Aside from whites' accounts, see *Walapai Ethnography*, pp. 183, 212-213, for two Walapais' stories of this incident, given in the late 1920s. Although the chief discussed above in the text was called Sherum and Tokoomhet in historical records, Dobyns and Euler, in *Wauba Yuma's People . . .*, show that the latter is the chiefly title rather than the particular man's name.

[99] Sheriff L. C. Welbourn to editor, Arizona City, September 18, 1872, in *Weekly Arizona Miner*, Sept. 28: see also issue of Sept. 14, 1872. One Mohave was killed, and the guilty party was no less than a captain, Choravi, or "Churoway." Yara tav intervened during the course of the negotiations.

Arizona tribes. It is unclear whether these efforts were directed ultimately against the eastern Apache, in the sense of helping to draw the whites' armaments away from western Arizona; or whether the idea was to attract the Tonto Apache within the peaceful zone, thus directing the whites' attention still further eastward against the eastern Apache bands with whom they were already at the point of final hostilities.[100] All this took more than six months to run its course, and it is hard to believe that Chooksa homar could not have known of it at the time. The process involved a number of full-dress visits and conferences, Maricopa coming to Fort Mohave, Yumas to Fort Mohave, Mohave talking to the Gila River tribes, and Mohave trips deep into Yavapai country. I cannot suggest why this most ambitious of all diplomatic efforts by Maricopa and Mohave together is not mentioned in this memoir.

One formal war expedition is altogether omitted from Chooksa homar's reminiscence, and that one was important enough to have made a fourteenth episode in his story if he had told it at all. That was the Mohave-Yuma-Yavapai expedition against the Maricopa in 1857, the very last of a ritualistic exchange of formal raids that had been going on for generations. It was altogether too grim an affair, too charged with national significance, simply to have fallen from memory. Even though Chooksa homar was little more than a child at the time he could hardly have failed to know, then or later, of this terrible disaster. The Mohave lost at least twice as many men in that attack as Chooksa homar would later see lying dead after the fight against Armistead.

It may be that Chooksa homar did talk about that expedition and that Kroeber omitted it from his notes, for some reason I cannot now guess at. But if Kroeber had left it out I feel sure that he would have noted the omission, as he did when passing by the kwohota's celebration in the first episode of this reminiscence. And other Mohave observed no taboo with regard to this expedition, since they spoke of it in later years to anthropologists.

So we are left to speculate why the expedition to the Gila does not appear in even the most veiled or passing reference. Perhaps this evokes once more the strongly individualistic attitude of the Mohave when telling his own story, within the scope of his tribal custom. Or perhaps Chooksa homar's own father died at Maricopa Wells in 1857, and he found this too painful to call into words after half a century.

---

[100] See Dodt to Andrews, and Andrews to General Stoneman, May 31 and June 4, 1870, in 734; King Woolsey's report of Juan Chivaria's request for his co-operation, Agua Caliente Ranch, June 20, 1870, in *Weekly Arizona Miner,* July 9, 1870; Capt. R. F. O'Beirne [commanding Camp Date Creek], letters of July 22, Aug. 4, and Oct. 26, in 393, and of Aug. 3 in *Weekly Arizona Miner* of Aug. 13, 1870; and Andrews to Commissioner, Sept. 6, 1870, in *Report, Indian Affairs, 1870,* p. 115, and of Sept. 30, in 734. Agent Helenus Dodt on the River Reservation stated that this affair (which he never did diagnose for what it was) had been apparent beginning in January of the year. The effort was overtaken by disruptive army pressure in the region, very late in 1870.

PLATES

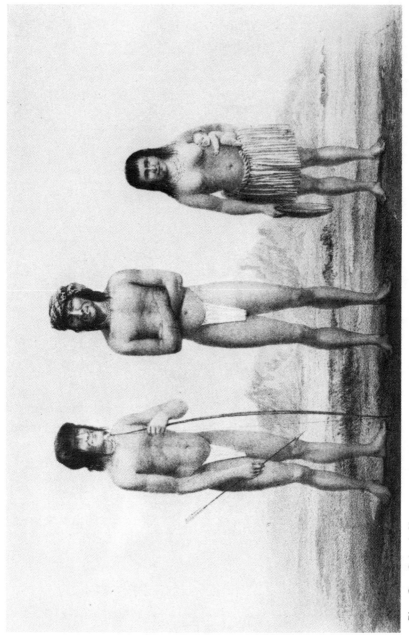

Plate One. Cairook, Yara tav, and unidentified Mohave Ms., pictured from life by H. B. Möllhausen in his capacity as artist with the expedition of Joseph C. Ives in 1857-1858: published in *Report upon the Colorado River of the West* . . . (Washington, D.C., 1861: 36 Cong 1 Sess H.E.D. 90, S.E.D. unnumbered).

Territory of Arizona,

Office of Superintendent of Indian Affairs,

La Paz Jany 1st 1867.

To all who shall see these presents, Greeting:

Know ye, that reposing special confidence in the integrity and discretion of "Ireta ba" Head Chief of the Mojave Indians (which position he has held under appointment from proper authority, since the occupancy of Arizona by Americans,) I do hereby recognise said "Iretaba" as Chief of the Mojave Indians and as such, commend him to Americans

Geo. W. Dent,
U.S. Superintendent of Indian Affairs for Territory of Arizona,

Plate Two. Confirmation of Yara tav as Chief of the Mohaves, referred to in the text as a controversial act by Superintendent of Indian Affairs George Dent. U.S. National Archives, Record Group 75, Microcopy 734, roll 2.

Plate Three. The promising young writer Frederick W. Loring, just back from the Wheeler Expedition and about forty hours before he was murdered near Wickenburg, Arizona Territory, by Yavapai Indians (November 5, 1871). T. H. O'Sullivan, photographer: copy in Bancroft Library, University of California, Berkeley, California.

Plate Four. Antonio Azul, Chief of the Pima and ally of the United States Army against the Apache, pictured in 1872 at about thirty years of age. Smithsonian Institution, National Anthropological Archives, Bureau of American Ethnology, negative 2611-A.

Plate Five. Juan Chivaria, war leader of the Maricopa. Smithsonian Institution, National Anthropological Archives, Bureau of American Ethnology, negative 52, 544.

Plate Six. At San Bernardino, California, on account of the incident mentioned in the text when Asukit gave up his son to white man's justice. Seated: Asukit and Each-a-what-thoo-may (Charlie Merriman), Mohaves. Standing: Dan Bunnell, W. I. Hancock, Dan Murphy, J. H. West, white men. Courtesy of Professor Lorraine M. Sherer who owns the photograph.

Plate Seven. Quichnailk (Jack Jones, Sr.), Mohave, interpreter for A. L. Kroeber in recording the reminiscence of Chooksa homar. Lowie Museum of Anthropology, University of California, Berkeley, negative 15-4311.

Plate Eight. Chooksa homar (Jo Nelson; Baby's Head), Mohave, narrator of the war reminiscence, when about sixty years of age. Lowie Museum of Anthropology, University of California, Berkeley, negative 15-2562.

Plate Nine. Kae-as-no-cum (Pascual), Chief of the Quechans, a New River Indian, in 1872 at about 72 years of age. United States Signal Corps photograph, no. 111-SC-87807, United States National Archives, Washington, D.C.

Plate Ten. Ah-hotch-o-cama, Western Yavapai band chief, and his fast friend Yara tav, a Mohave chief, shaman, and kwanami, pictured at some time between late 1863 or early 1864 (when Yara tav was given the uniform) and September, 1865 (when he surrendered it in a Chemehuevi ambush). The photograph was Arthur Woodward's and is reproduced here by kind permission of Paul D. Bailey, publisher of Woodward's *Feud on the Colorado,* in which book the picture appears.